One Youth Pastor's
TOOLBOX

By Ryan Rench

Copyright © 2016 by:
Ryan Rench and Calvary Baptist Publications of Temecula, CA.

All Scripture quotations are taken from the King James Version.

All rights reserved. No part of this publication may be reproduced, distributed, or transmitted in any form or by any means, including photocopying, recording, or other electronic or mechanical methods, without the prior written permission of the publisher, except in the case of brief quotations embodied in critical reviews and certain other noncommercial uses permitted by copyright law. For permission requests, write to the publisher, addressed "Attention: Permissions Coordinator," at the address below.

CALVARY BAPTIST PUBLICATIONS
TEMECULA, CA | CALVARYBAPTIST.PUB

Calvary Baptist Church | Pastor W. M. Rench
31087 Nicolas Rd. Temecula, CA 92591
(951) 676-8700 | cbctemecula.org

Contents

Introduction 1

1. Sermon Series 3

Sunday School Series 4
Romans – "The Just Shall Live by Faith" 4
Daniel – "God Rules. So It's God's Rules." 4
1 Corinthians – "CLEAN UP! And Here's How..." 5
Proverbs – "What Is the Wise Thing to Do?" 5

Wednesday Night Series 7
Guest Speakers 7
Man Time/Lady Time 7
Outreach Training 8
BIBS: Big Idea Bible Study 8
Gender Series 11
Baptist Series 12
The Tongue 12
Teens of Faith Series 13

2. Activities 20

Progressive Dinner 20
Scavenger Hunt (Picture/Video) 20
Ice Skating/Johns Incredible Pizza 21
Camping Overnight 21
MORP – Because Baptists Don't Do Prom! 21
Grad Sunday 21
Promotion Sunday 21
"Open House," SNAC (Sunday Nights After Church), or Afterglows ... 22
Theme Park 22
Water Day 22
Beach Bash 22
Youth Rallies 22
Bonfire Night 23
Christmas Party 23

3. Big Trips 25

Church Planters Conference (January) 25
Heartland Road Trip/College Days (April) 25
Missions Trips (June) 26
Summer Camp (July) 26
Winter Camp (December) 26

4. Games 27

Using the Teens to Run the Game Times 27

Active Small Assembly Games (10-40 People) 29

One-Chair Musical Chairs 29
Hold The Spit! 29
Floor Pong 29
Round Robin Table Tennis 30
Game of Letters 30
Do You Love Your Neighbor? 31
Death Ball 31
Number Groups 32

Non-Active Small Assembly Games (10-40 People) 33

Sword Drills 33
9-Square Tic Tac Toe 33
Mafia 33
Contact 34
Boppity Bop Bop Bop 35
Big Bang 36
Signs 37
Head Moose 37
PSST 38
Couch (Also called "Four On the Couch") 39

Up Front Games (Large Assembly) 41

Total Blackout 41
2014 Preaching Rally: 42

Outdoor Games 44

Ninja 44
One-Pitch Softball 44
Outpost 45

Time Killers 47

My Fishy 47

  Throw the Ball 47
  I'm Going On Vacation 47
  Johnny Whoop! 47
  9+6=3 48
  Around the World 48
  Where Are You Going Next? 48
  Green Glass Door 48
  This Is a Pen 49
  Twenty Sick Sheep 49
  Wednesday 49
  Coffin 49
  Hole 49

5. Fundraisers 51

  Comedy Night 51
  Yard Sale 53
  Cookies (With Donation Bucket) 53
  Table Tennis Tournament 53

6. Various Youth Ideas 55

  Youth Philosophy 55
  Preaching Rally 56
  Youth Nights 64
  Announcement Sheets 65
  Self Report Cards 66
  Future Plans 67
  Game Room 67
  Camp T-Shirts 68
  Tape Measure Questions 70
  Calendars 70
  Wednesday "Big Day" 72
  Homiletics 74

7. Books 75

Christian/Ministry 76

  Knowing God 76
  The Courage to Be Protestant 77
  The Pursuit of God 77
  I Am a Church Member 77
  Love and Respect 78

    Biblical Youth Work 78
    Purposeful Parenting 78
    Forward in The Face of Fear 79
    The Case for The Resurrection 81
    Off Script 81
    Pilgrim's Progress 82
    Book Loaning Night 82

Preaching Books 85
    A Man of God 85
    Biblical Preaching 86
    Invitation to Biblical Preaching 87
    Living by the Book 87
    Preaching with Freshness 87
    The Art and Craft of Biblical Preaching 88
    Why Johnny Can't Preach 88

Bible Study (Software) 89
    BestCommentaries.com 89
    Olive Tree Bible App 89
    KJV with Strong's References 90

Calvary Baptist Publications 91
    The Preaching Rally 91
    BIBS: Big Idea Bible Study 93
    BIBS Devotional: One-Year 94
    BIBS Devotional: Proverbs 95
    Interning Well 96
    A Case for Being Timeless 97
    Love God, Love Others, Do Right 98
    A Case for Bible College 98
    "A Case for..." Minibooks 100
    Encourage Your Pastor 101
    Booklets By Pastor W. M. Rench 102

Gender 104
    Why Gender Matters 104
    Girls On the Edge 104
    Boys Adrift 105

Leadership – Historical 106
    Up from Slavery 106
    Character Building 107
    R. E. Lee On Leadership 107

    The Second World War: Milestones to Disaster 108
    Personal Memoirs of U. S. Grant 109

Leadership – Modern 110
    Extreme Ownership 110
    EntreLeadership 110
    Tribes 111
    Good Leaders Ask Great Questions 111

Historical Narrative 112
    Unbroken 112
    1776 112
    Endurance: Shackleton's Incredible Voyage 113
    The Wright Brothers 113

Writing 114
    The Elements of Style 114
    Story Grid 114
    APE: Author Publisher Entrepreneur 115
    Your First 1000 Copies 115

Personal Growth 116
    The Power of Habit 116
    Linchpin 116
    How to Fail at Almost Everything and Still Win Big 117
    Quiet 117
    The One Thing 118
    The Shallows 118
    Simple Rules 119

Business Principles 120
    The Thank You Economy 120
    Platform 120
    Will It Fly? 121

Finances 122
    Smart Money, Smart Kids 122
    Foundations in Personal Finance 122
    The Millionaire Mind and The Millionaire Next Door 123

8. Websites 125

Bible Study 125
Christian Helps 126
    CalvaryBaptist.pub 126

    RyanRench.com 126
    TheHeartlandConnect.com 127
Miscellaneous Favorites 128
    SafeSmartSocial.com 128
    Unroll.Me 129
    16Personalities.com 130
    StrengthFinder.com 131
    VidAngel.com 133

9. Podcasts 135

I Listen Regularly to: 135
    Youth Ministry Life 135
    Story Grid 135
    Poddy Break 136
    Smart Passive Income 136
    The Idea Talks 137
    Dave Ramsey Show 137
    Andy Stanley Leadership 137
    Thom Rainer On Leadership 138

I Listen Occasionally to: 139
    This Is Your Life 139
    ChurchMag Podcast 139
    EntreLeadership 139
    The Tech Guy 140
    48 Days to the Work You Love 140

10. Various Ministry Ideas 141

    Focus... Is It a Dirty Word in Ministry? 141
Lesson Notes 143
    Finance Sermon 143
    Co-Op "Catechism" Class 153
Ministry Tools 157
    Throwable Microphone 157
    Apple TV 157
    Digital Encouragement File 158
Interns 159

11. Other Random Stuff 161
Medi-Share 161
FBA – Fulfillment by Amazon 163
Virtual Assistants 166

12. Management Tools 169
Communication 169
Slack 169
Trello 170
IFTTT 170
FaceTime (or Skype, or Google Hangout) 171
Jing (Or QuickTime screen capture) 171
Capture/Organize 172
Evernote 172
Inbox 172
File Sharing 174
Google Drive 174
Dropbox 175
LastPass 175
Scanner Pro (by Readdle) 176
Genius Scan 176
Email Management Ideas 177
Inbox Zero 177
Gmail 177
Multiple Inboxes 178
Keyboard Shortcuts 179

Introduction

A youth pastor is necessarily a multifarious individual. One day, he's crafting a sermon like a 17th century scholar; the next, he's crafting dodge ball rules like a junior high gym coach. As an associate pastor, he might be a song-leader, a counselor, an IT guy or a janitor. Maybe all four. And more.

With so many interests, some people might call him scatter-brained. I prefer the term *well-rounded.* It makes *me* feel better, anyway. I am one of those... things. A youth pastor.

Every year, I attend a gathering of the greatest minds of the galaxy (er, at least we think so) to discuss youth ministry topics. We meet for three days, and each ministry leader brings ideas that they have tried in their respective ministries.

I rip off their ideas (pretending they're mine), test them on my teens (lab rats), write up the results and share them the following year. This book is an adaptation of those notes.

The toolbox in my garage at home is packed with a random assortment of all my favorite and essential tools. That's what this book is—my essential and favorite ministry tools. I use some of these tools every day. Some, every week. Others, only once in a while. Not every tool is great, but they all serve some purpose. I even include a few tools that *did not* work for me, but might for you.

Use what you like, as is. It is probably not original with me, so feel free to pretend it was your idea. I do it all the time.

Adapt what you do not like. Make it work for you.

Finally, ignore the rest, for now. File it in your brain in your "someday/maybe" reference list, and return to it later, when you're bone-dry desperate for any—ANY—idea that some bozo has used before. That's when I come through best… when all the good ideas have already been used up.

Enjoy.

(I repeatedly demand that my teens call me "the Pope of Temecula." They smirk and pat my bald spot with a condescending "There, there, Brother Ryan…" I'm the bigger man. I don't get mad. I'll accept "youth pastor" instead.)

Ryan Rench, Calvary Baptist Church, Temecula, CA

1. Sermon Series

In our youth department, we have two separate class times: Sunday school and Wednesday night. I have historically used Sundays for preaching through books of the Bible and Wednesdays for specific topics. Simple, clear, weekly preaching through the Bible is what we do for our Sunday school hour. Our Sunday school is more formal than our Wednesday nights and lends itself toward the subjects taught this way.

So far in my short (six-year) preaching career I have made it through four books of the Bible: Romans, Daniel, 1 Corinthians and Proverbs (and a couple sermons on Philemon, if you want to count that as a series), as well as several topical series.

With each new series, I purchase the most conservative, highest-rated and most recommended commentary I can find (in addition to using the ones I already own). Whatever your philosophy on commentaries, the fact remains that they provide an outside perspective on the text, including history, grammar and an opinion on the interpretation of the text.

This chapter explains some of the series we have worked through. For ANY of my sermon notes (manuscript outlines) covering any of these topics, *please contact me directly through my website at RyanRench.com*. This section is listed in date order.

Sunday School Series

Romans – "The Just Shall Live by Faith"

As my introductory series, I wanted the Romans series to be a launching point for our young people to become teens of faith. I wanted the principles of *saving faith* and *growing faith* to permeate every sermon of the series, and knew that the books of Romans would include great preaching for both saved and unsaved people.

The series went directly through each verse of the book, and covered the five major movements including Condemnation (1-3), Salvation (3-5), Sanctification (6-8), Dispensation (9-11) and Application (12-16).

Mini-series emerged from within the overall series, covering topics like spiritual gifts and living in the Spirit. The series was 78 sermons long.

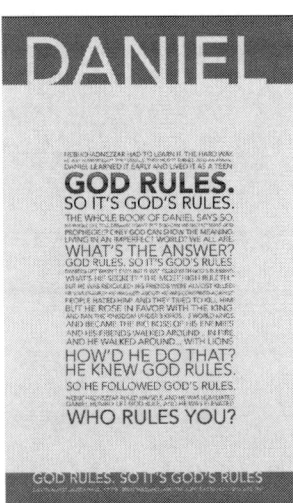

Daniel – "God Rules. So It's God's Rules."

Daniel is a fascinating Bible character with an astounding book named after him. Daniel never knew the end of his stories, yet he always chose to live for God. This series was a constant reminder that God is the ruler among men, so He has the right to be *our* ruler. The stories of the first half of the book are convicting to any Christian, and the history/prophecy of the second half of the book is a gripping study. While some of the sermons were deep, at times, I worked to always apply the Word to the teens' lives so that it could help them spiritually in some way. The series was 30 sermons long.

Resources. I drew from my college notes written by Professor Ed Pearson at Heartland Baptist Bible College, as well as our class textbook—the commentary on Daniel by John Phillips. In addition, I used the *NAC Vol. 18 – Daniel* commentary by Stephen Miller. This Daniel commentary is technical and concise, yet applicable blending devotional content with technical accuracy. It is theologically conservative, and I agree with most of its teachings.

1 Corinthians – "CLEAN UP! And Here's How…"

This series through 1 Corinthians was a hard-hitting letter on how quickly a good church can allow sin to infiltrate and spoil it like leaven. Each chapter of the book exposes some new sin and provides God's clear answer to it. The main thrust of the overall series was that although God denounces sin, he always provides the answer of how best to clean it up. Seventy sermons covered topics including dating, church membership, spiritual gifts, the resurrection, communion, faithfulness and more.

Resources. Although I drew from several sources, I largely consulted *New International Commentary On the New Testament: First Corinthians,* by Gordon Fee. Considered a Bible expert, Dr. Fee is a renowned author known especially for this book and the college classes he taught around it. While I had to skip some of his sections on sign gifts, I found his overall approach masterful. He found Paul's heart and mind as he wrote to the Corinthians, and uncovered Paul's motives line by line through this commentary. I appreciated Dr. Fee's approach throughout the book, always explaining the reason each text was originally written.

Proverbs – "What Is the Wise Thing to Do?"

Our most recent Sunday series took a look at this question, "What is the wise thing to do?" I was listening to a podcast that asked the same question, and I thought that question would be an easy way to describe Proverbs. Not surprisingly, each sermon came back to the essential choice between wisdom or selfishness.

Proverbs is simple to explain and easy to apply to teens. It was written to young people, so every warning in Proverbs is applicable to teens and applies to a variety of topics. I preached only a few highlight verses from each chapter and spent more than 50 sermons in the series.

Resources. *The NIV Application Commentary Proverbs* by Paul Koptak. While I personally do not use the NIV Bible (I use the KJV exclusively in my personal study and church ministry), I have found this commentary set to be helpful. I have purchased the Proverbs and Ephesians Volumes from this set, and each have been well formatted. Each chapter is outlined in three sections: Original Meaning, Bridging Contexts, and Contemporary Significance. The Original Meaning section is helpful to understand the author's intent, and it is the most helpful section of the commentary, in my opinion.

Bridges Commentary On Proverbs. As part of the Crossway Classic Commentaries set, this book provides valuable insights into the book of Proverbs. It is not overly technical and reads similarly to a Spurgeon or Matthew Henry book, although the content goes a bit deeper. It is a helpful resource for a classic look at certain texts, although it may not answer some of the tougher questions you might have regarding a particular text.

Wednesday Night Series

Guest Speakers

Churches are filled with people whose lives have been changed by Jesus Christ. The men and ladies of my church have interesting stories, and I want our young people to be exposed to the stories of the people they worship with weekly. We occasionally have a series of guest speakers from our church to share their testimonies with the teens.

In gender split classes we have had moms share some of the struggles they went through as teens, or elderly ladies share decades of wisdom with our young ladies. The men of our church give their advice through testimony times, or by filling the pulpit when I am gone. Some of the greatest connections within our church have come through the men and ladies of our church sharing their stories.

Each summer, our two interns each preach a series. This provides an alternate voice from a passionate young man, and our teens respond well to their influence each summers.

Man Time/Lady Time

For a few-months season, in lieu of our opening time of games and announcements, we did a practical time of training for the men and the ladies. It usually lasted about 15 or 20 minutes and included various life-experience topics listed below (one topic per week):

Man-time

- APPEARANCE: Matching clothes (styles, colors, etc.), shining shoes, hygiene, etc.
- HOW TO: tie a tie, write a thank-you note, jump a car battery, shoot a basketball, play volleyball, tie knots, shake hands, remember names, have proper flag etiquette, build a fire, sew a button, etc.

- GUEST SPEAKERS: various church members
- DATING/GENDER: gender roles, dating principles, etc.
- MISCELLANEOUS: general etiquette

Lady-time

- APPEARANCE: makeup, hair, cleanliness, clothing (colors, matching, etc.)
- HOW TO: sewing tips, cooking tips, meal planning, cleaning tips, etc.
- GUEST SPEAKERS: various church members
- DATING/GENDER: gender roles, dating principles, etc.
- MISCELLANEOUS: CPR overview, first aid, general etiquette, etc.

Outreach Training

Our teens were coming to door-knocking but rarely had soul-winning interactions. This series included memory verses and an outreach plan from start to finish that we adapted from my time at Bible Baptist Church in Stillwater, OK. The series covered about 15 weeks.

BIBS: Big Idea Bible Study

It started with a Bible Study Series. Then a daily devotional. Then a Christian School curriculum. Then a book called *BIBS: Big Idea Bible Study*.

After teaching several weeks on the general topic of the Bible (Bible preaching, Bible study, Bible history, etc.), I then taught several weeks on *how* to study the Bible.

I taught from a couple key resources:

- Haddon Robinson's *Biblical Preaching*
- Howard Hendricks' *Living by the Book*

I tried to drill this thought into their brains: "What is God saying?"

- Do not start with "What is God saying <u>to me</u>." Start with the reason God said it in the first place.
- Author intent is huge in Bible interpretation.

The three overall principles of Bible study are:

- Observation – birds-eye view
- Interpretation – what is God saying?
- Application – what is God saying to me?

An example of the BIBS process is as follows:

Psalm 117:1-2 O praise the Lord, all ye nations: praise him, all ye people. 2. For his merciful kindness is great toward us: and the truth of the Lord endureth for ever. Praise ye the Lord.

Observation. We know little about the Psalm itself, but because it is a Psalm, we understand that it is directed to God, or written about God.

Interpretation (the BIBS steps)

- **Read and reread the text**. Done. Did not take long.
- **Flag words**. I understand all the words, but looking up certain words adds depth to my understanding.
    - V2 – *Great*. Prevail. Have strength. Mighty. Confirm. Give Strength.
    - V2 – *Endureth for ever*. Everlasting. Eternal. Unending future.
- **Word**. Praise
- **Phrase**. Praise the Lord
- **Sentence**. We should praise the Lord.
- **Question Word**. Why?
- **Question**. Why should we praise the Lord?
- **Answers**: 1) His merciful kindness and 2) His truth endures.

- **Big Idea**. We should praise the Lord because His mercy is great toward us and His truth endures forever.

(See book **BIBS: Big Idea Bible Study** Appendix for more details and further examples.)

BIBS DEVOTIONALS. We developed and printed our own daily devotional books based on what we had been teaching through on Wednesday nights. We call them: *BIBS – Big Idea Bible Study Daily Devotional*.

The BIBS format is designed to provide both the depth of Scripture study as well as the broad, sweeping overviews and author's flow of thought, and the devotional reinforces both principles daily. Each day, you read a large portion of Scripture (usually 2-3 chapters) in order to maintain the birds-eye view. In addition, you work on interpreting a smaller portion of Scripture (usually 5-15 verses or so) based on the natural text divisions.

BIBS could be described as homiletics in a devotional form. If homiletics is writing a *sermon* that represents a boiled-down idea that is communicated through preaching, why should not our daily *devotions* be that too: a boiled-down idea that God is communicating through His Word?

Application Days. After working through both the observation and interpretation, the student then spends two days per week on application—the part I emphasize the most.

The student does not work for the "right answer," they work to hear from God through His Word. The application pages each week (Sunday and Wednesday) ask for 1) General principles learned from the previous days' study, 2) Specific applications of the Big Idea, and 3) What they plan to *do* differently based on what they've been hearing from God. (e.g. if the Big Idea was: "Daniel stood by faith even when the penalty was death" they would apply it as "Since I won't even be threatened by death like Daniel, I can stand by faith in school by taking my Bible, speaking up in tomorrow's class debates about abortion, passing out 3 gospel tracts to John, Sally, and Fred and pray for my meal at lunchtime.")

WEDNESDAY NIGHT CLASS DISCUSSION. The classes split by gender and have a discussion from their BIBS. Each week is a recap over what they had been studying all week and a discussion of their interpretation and application.

I was careful to balance teaching and discussion time so as not to ignore their input, but also present the correct interpretation! This was NOT a "share how this text makes you feel" or "what do you think about this text" session. It was carefully guided so as to correctly present the proper interpretation of Scripture.

When it came to application, lots of various input came in. We spend about 35-45 minutes of class discussion on BIBS.

RESULTS. I have told the teens that whether they realize it or not, the BIBS series has produces more spiritual growth than anything else we have done. They have not only become more and more disciplined to figure out first what God is saying to them (interpretation), but they are learning the necessary next step of making it mean something to themselves personally (application)!

This is the only series I have ever repeated. It is my favorite format for personal Bible study, and it is simple enough that almost anyone can do it. The series covered several months each time.

Gender Series

Borrowing much from my former pastor, the Gender Series dove into various aspects of being 100% masculine and 100% feminine. Contrasting the gender positions of Genesis 1 to Romans 1 shows that the differences between the two are taken in steps. This was a Wednesday night series done in three sections:

BIBLICAL – we started with the biblical foundations for gender and expanded it to the biblical roles of what their lives would be as male and female. For most of them it would be husband or wife, and we taught through much of the roles of gender.

PRACTICAL – after the biblical basis was laid, we went through some practical applications, reviewing the Bible basis each week but spending more time on application. Topics included looking, thinking, and acting like a man or lady; and we put in a few split sessions for men/ladies.

DATING – not wanting to overemphasize this point, we only spent a few weeks talking about the biblical basis for dating, or by some definitions, courtship. We emphasized the biblical guidelines of purity and marriage, and taught that anything outside those guidelines are not wise.

After 20 sermons, we concluded the series with a message I stole from Pastor Jason Gaddis titled "Ice Cream Sundae Relationships:"

- The Bowl – spiritual foundation is the most important
- Ice Cream – the bulk of the relationship should be the friendship
- Syrup – the intellectual and relational aspect fills the gaps and covers all
- Whipped Cream – the emotional part is fluffy and unsubstantial, but sweet
- Cherry – the last and the smallest aspect of a relationship is physical, which comes only after marriage

To download a free trifold brochure that illustrates each of these steps, visit RyanRench.com/icecream

Baptist Series

Starting with a biblical basis for the church and developing the idea of authority, we spent several weeks preaching through various passages relating to this progression of authority: God's authority> Jesus> church> other churches. From this series came the booklet titled *A Case for "Church."*

After the month on authority we spent the next couple months going through Baptist distinctives notes. These were weekly, detailed fill-in-the-blank notes that we printed and handed out each week. We went through it quickly but clearly. The whole series (church and Baptist) lasted only about 12 weeks.

The Tongue

In between series I taught a 4-week series on the tongue.

- CLOSE your mouth (Shut Up) – Prov. 17:27-28
- OPEN your mouth (Speak Up) – Ephesians 4:17-32
- WATCH your mouth (Watch It) – James 3
- USE your mouth (Use It) – rebuke, soul winning, spiritual gifts.

To view a handout of verses from Proverbs relating to each topic, visit RyanRench.com/Proverbs

Teens of Faith Series

Explanation: We have done a Wednesday night preaching series answering the question, "What does it mean to be a teen of faith?" Our youth department "theme verses" are Romans 1:16-17, *"For I am not ashamed of the gospel of Christ: for it is the power of God unto salvation to every one that believeth; to the Jew first, and also to the Greek.*[17] *For therein is the righteousness of God revealed from faith to faith: as it is written, The just shall live by faith."* The key concept of the series was that a Christian is a picture of God's righteousness as he lives by the same faith in which he was saved. The theme tagline is "Saving faith. Growing faith." It is ALL faith in Christ.

So, when we are living by faith in Christ... what does it look like?

A saying I often use in writing notes or in preaching is, "Love God. Love others. Do right." This has become a mantra of ours, and I believe it sums up much of what the Christian life should look like.

Because teens are at the first stages of learning to make decisions (moving out of childhood), they, more than any other group in the church, need *specific* instructions on *what* to do. They might hear the concept, but most teens do not think in principles yet. Rather than preach *only* principles as broad concepts (e.g. "loving God"), the Teens of Faith series is an in-depth look at what it means to *live* as a teen of faith. Each week we explore a different aspect of the three main headings, as outlined below.

Topics: Our "Love God. Love others. Do right." mantra serves as the outline to the Teens of Faith series. Under each heading falls several topics. Most topics are covered in one lesson each, while some take a series. Each lesson is practical and gives some step-by-step instruction, inspiration and examples. Large 4' x 5' posters (pictured) were hung to reinforce the messages.

LOVING GOD

Learning to daily fall more in love with God because of all that He's done for us.

A LOT OF PROBLEMS COULD be solved in life if we as Christians obeyed the first commandment as we should. God has done so much for us that it only makes sense for us to live in humble gratitude.

In the Teens of Faith we desire a passion that drives us to fall deeper and deeper in love with our Savior. Every week, at least some aspect is encouraged in growing our love for our Lord, and a lot falls under this "big umbrella:"

daily devotions • church attendance • family relationships • hunger for preaching • passion about church services • driving motivation to grow • Bible memory • attitude • spirit

LOVING GOD – *Learning to daily fall more in love with God because of all He's done for us.*

- Love God by lifting Him up – Matthew 22:34-40
- Love God wholly – Mark 12:30
- Love God by loving His house – various passages: Romans 1:13-17 compared with Romans 16:25-27; *A Case for Sunday Evening Church* minibook; Psalm 122:1; Hebrews 10:25; 1 Corinthians 3:16 (house of God); 4th commandment (Lord's day)
- Love God by loving His Word (multiple weeks)
    - *Evidence that Demands a Verdict* workbook (3 weeks)
    - *BIBS* workbook (3 weeks)
    - Journaling
    - Memorization
    - Learning to listen, love and apply preaching
- HOW to love God (workbook – multiple weeks)
    - How to FALL in love with God
        - Remember God – 1 John 4:19
        - Turn to God – 1 Samuel 7:2-3
    - How to STAY in love with God
        - Fellowship with God (Psalm 37:4-5; John 15)
        - Stay with God – Deuteronomy 13:1-4
- Love God by loving your family
    - Ephesians 6
    - 5th commandment
    - Generational parenting
    - Marriage
    - Proverbs – instruction to children
- Love God by talking with Him (lesson on prayer) – various passages: James 5; 1 Thessalonians 5; Daniel 9; Matthew 26:36-50; Mark 14:32-46; Luke 22:39-49; John 18:1; John 18:2

LOVING OTHERS

Letting our love for God overflow into our everyday love for every person around us.

TO SAY THAT YOU HAVE a sincere, passionate love for God and still harbor bitterness or hatred for someone means that you're lying. Wow! That's coming out strong! But it's true. (1 Jn. 4:20) Basically everything in the whole Bible boils down to 1) do you love God, and 2) do you love others. (Mat. 22:40)

Your love for others shows up a lot of different ways. Here are a few things we encourage in the Teens of Faith:

outreach • soul-winning • door knocking • encouraging others to come on activities • absentee followup • greeting classmates and welcoming guests • new 7th grader assimilation and welcome • mentoring • not gossiping • not being bitter or hateful

LOVING OTHERS – *Letting our love for God overflow into our everyday love for every person around us.*

- Love others intro – Matthew 22:34-40, Mark 12:28-34
- Promotion Sunday – new 7th graders (Good Samaritan – who are you being a good neighbor to?) – Luke 10:25-37
- Assimilating/mentoring others – Romans 13:8-10
- Loving those who cannot repay, or who do not deserve your love – Philemon
- "Be Our Guest:" getting over our fear of strangers and greeting class guests in order to show them love – 1 John 4
- Spiritual gifts: encouraging others – 1 Corinthians 12, Romans 12
- Love God by not hating others. By harboring no bitterness. By making things right – 1 John 2:3-11 (9-11)
- Loving everyone, like Christ loves us – Romans 5:1-8
- Outreach series (12 weeks)
- Outreach videos (4 weeks through 30-minute video intros to lessons)
    - "Noah" – noahthemovie.com (NOT the Russell Crowe version)
    - "Genius" – geniusthemovie.com (using the Beatles as a witnessing tool)
    - "180" – 180movie.com (important discussions on abortion used as witnessing tool)
    - "Evolution vs. God" – evolutionvsGod.com (interviews with evolutionists as witnessing tool
- We love others because Christ loved us – 1 John 4:11-21
- Love others by sacrificing (like Christ laid down his life) – 1 John 3:16
- Loving others (wrap-up sermon) – John 13:34-35, 1 John 2:7

DOING RIGHT

Genuinely loving God and others so much that it shows in how we live day by day.

YOU CAN SERVE GOD WITHOUT loving Him, but you can't love God without serving Him. A heart that is absolutely full and overflowing with gratitude for all God's blessings can't help but love others too. When that love for God and others grows, a mature Christian cannot help but let it affect everything about his life. He MUST serve. He MUST help others. He MUST learn to be the biggest blessing that he can be. A few ideas of "doing right" in the Teens of Faith are:

serving • applying passionately listening • blessing to others • to be asked • speak preaching • removing sin from our lives • to preaching • actively looking for ways to be a seeing the need, taking the lead • not waiting helping • volunteering • ing out against wrong and for right

DOING RIGHT – *Genuinely loving God and others so much that is shows in how we live day by day.*

- Obey God's commands – John 15
- Love God by doing right. Love God by obeying his commandments. (They are not grievous) – 1 John 5:1-3
- Love God by doing right in deed and truth – 1 John 3:18
- Be God's workmanship – Ephesians 2:10, Titus 3:9
- Faith is shown (proved) through works – James 2
- Giving – 2 Corinthians 9:7
- Serving – Luke 17:10
- Keep *love* as the essence of the *doing* – 1 Corinthians 13, Romans 12:9
- Fear God and keep his commandments – Ecclesiastes 12:13-14

2. Activities

Note: I do ALL of these activities almost annually. These are not ideas that I have not tried, but ones that I use and love. For any further details on any of our activities (including some of our more turn-key, detailed After Action Reports), contact me directly! These are roughly in date order.

Progressive Dinner

Set up various stops, black out the windows on the bus and progress through each phase of dinner (appetizer, salad, bread, main course, dessert, etc.) The stops can be fast food restaurants, grocery stores, or church members' homes.

Scavenger Hunt (Picture/Video)

Divide your group into smaller groups of 4-5, give each group an adult chaperone/driver and a list of items in your town, and send them off for 1.5 hours. Each item on the list is given points based on how far from church it is, and special bonuses are awarded for various tasks like "Have your whole team in the picture." Subtract points for *every minute* they are past your deadline, and then compile their pictures into team slideshows once they arrive (they can snack while you prepare the simple slideshow).

Ice Skating/Johns Incredible Pizza

Take the teens ice skating, then have lunch at a big arcade pizza buffet like John's Incredible Pizza.

Camping Overnight

Take the teens to a campsite for a 2-day getaway to play organized games (volleyball, kickball, etc.) and provide free time for them to play together. For us, the campsite provides the meals and activities, and we bring our own tents and other materials. We have several group devotional times (evening, morning, and afternoon), and have every minute clearly defined on their schedules.

MORP – Because Baptists Don't Do Prom!

Around the time of prom, provide a banquet for the teens to attend. We have done themed nights (i.e. "nerd night"), progressive dinners, a CLUE night and mystery dinners, for example.

To read a letter I sent to parents regarding prom, see ryanrench.com/prom.

Grad Sunday

Each year, our church honors our graduates with a personalized Bible and an opportunity to present a display table and give a testimony in church. Cake is served outside after the service.

Promotion Sunday

Each year, we ceremoniously receive our new 7th graders with applause and excitement on our Promotion Sunday. Since it is a big step going from 6th grade to 7th grade, we teach our teens to ease the tension and receive the newest 7th graders lovingly.

"Open House," SNAC (Sunday Nights After Church), or Afterglows

Open your home to the teens on Sunday nights after church for the summer. We provide snacks or a light meal (cereal, ham & cheese sandwiches, etc.) and let the teens hang out in the garage playing floor pong (see chapter 4 – Games), building Legos, constructing marble tracks, playing foosball, etc. Occasionally, we do this at a church member's home for a shorter amount of time.

Theme Park

Take the teens to a theme park on a group rate. Even if they have a park close by, they rarely get all their friends together to go at the same time, so a youth activity is a good time to make memories together with Christian friends. We attend Knott's Berry Farm in Orange County, CA (our 6 Flags is pretty run down and over 2 hours away.)

Water Day

Lay out a 50' x 100' plastic tarp, douse it with children's soap (in case it is ingested or gets in their eyes), turn on the hose and sprinklers and play some games! We played giant slip-and-slide games like steal the bacon, American Eagle, fill the bucket and more.

Beach Bash

Take the teens to the beach in the evening for a hot dog roast, Frisbee football, American Eagle and campfire testimonies a few weeks after summer camp (sorry, non-coastal youth groups!)

Youth Rallies

When the schedule permits, attend another church's youth rally for a day of games and preaching. As a youth pastor, all you have to do is drive a bus for this activity!

Bonfire Night

Have an evening hayride, a simple soup meal, and outdoor activity to play nighttime capture-the-flag, freeze tag, and other night games. A campfire marshmallow roast and testimony time completes the evening.

Christmas Party

Meet at the youth pastor's house for an evening of silly indoor games (like Minute-To-Win-It or a Tacky Sweater Photo Contest), snacks, a $5 gift exchange, and a Christmas spiritual challenge for the new year.

3. Big Trips

Note: We take a few main trips throughout the course of the year. Some trips are annual, and others are only as we have teens interested.

Church Planters Conference (January)

Our church attends the Church Planting Conference hosted by Heartland Baptist Bible College each year. We fly to OKC and arrange our own lodging. The Church Planters Conference is a gathering of almost 100 church planters from all over America, and scores of other pastors and ministry workers who come to give money for the needs of the church planters. It is a great conference that our teens and church members love to attend.

Heartland Road Trip/College Days (April)

Take a college survey road trip with your upperclassmen who are at least considering God's direction for their lives. We partnered with another church to make the trip affordable and more fun, and we trekked across I-40 from California to Oklahoma to visit Heartland Baptist Bible College in Oklahoma City. On the way out, we visited the Grand Canyon and took a leisurely pace. We slept in churches for free and ate simple meals and snacks. Taking a 20-hour road trip might seem intimidating, but the bonding on the bus ride is priceless.

Missions Trips (June)

Domestic or foreign missions trips are great opportunities to 1) EXPOSE your teens to places outside their own sphere of life, and 2) ENCOURAGE church planters and missionaries around the world. Our church has only done two so far—Alaska and Los Angeles—but we plan on going overseas in the future. The Alaska Missions Trip exposed our young people to rural poverty-stricken village ministries with rampant sexual and substance abuse. The Inner City Los Angeles Church Planting Missions Trip exposed our young people to the millions of souls in inner cities, and the effects of sin seen in the streets and homeless shelters.

Summer Camp (July)

The most important week in our summer is youth camp. We help as many students as possible go to camp, supporting them financially and encouraging them to sign up early. Since camp is a sheltered spiritual environment with its main focus on the preaching of God's Word, I view camp as a potent "shot" of spiritual growth.

Winter Camp (December)

Right around New Year's Day, our group heads to the mountains for a 2-night winter camp. We combine with other churches for fun games, a relaxed environment, and at least four preaching sessions. Winter camp is a more laid back environment than summer camp, yet making good memories together is an equally important spiritual benefit.

4. Games

Note: We play almost all of these games regularly.

Using the Teens to Run the Game Times

I allow our teens to run every Wednesday night's game time. We play for about 20 minutes before the announcement and preaching time, and the teens choose, prepare, and run the games.

Here was my original post to them:

> ***EVER WANTED TO CHOOSE AND RUN OUR WEDNESDAY NIGHT GAMES? NOW YOU CAN!***
>
> *I've got a crazy idea... how about YOU choose and run the games on Wednesday nights. Here's how this is going to work...*
>
> **We'll assemble a team or teams.** *Add your name to the signup sheet in the back if you are interested in helping with this. Each team will have only 2-4 people on it.*
>
> **We'll schedule your team's night.** *Once you have your team, you will be given a schedule of when your night to do the games is. This might be every week (if there's only one team), or it might be once per month. It all depends on who signs up.*
>
> **You will plan your game.** *Meet with your team to plan a game for everyone. It can be a big deal (like a month-long running contest with points and teams and outdoor*

adventures and indoor puzzles... whatever!), or it can be simple (like Bible tic-tac-toe or Sword Drills). Seriously!

We'll discuss your game. *Once your team's game is planned, let me know the week before so it can be approved. We do not want the same game 3 weeks in a row, and we do not always want the same kinds of games, so we will discuss your ideas and approve each one.*

You'll run your game! *On your night, YOU will run the game. You'll prepare all the props ahead of time, you'll explain any rules, etc. This is YOUR night, so make it amazing. Or simple. Whatever you prefer.*

Let me know if you are interested by signing up. This will be fun!

-Bro. Ryan

It has been working fabulously!

- It relieves me from having to plan and organize the games
- It teaches them responsibility
- They are all into it, because THEY planned it!

I designated one of the teen girls to schedule out the teams and get with them on games, reminding them to tell me the week before. She does a great job, posting the teams on the white board and always scheduling a month out.

We have had great games, including Family Feud, a Christian Veggie Tales Karaoke Contest, PSST, Death Ball, and more. I completely recommend it, although it takes some oversight.

Active Small Assembly Games (10-40 People)

One-Chair Musical Chairs

Ideal for 10+ people in each group; separate men from ladies. Arrange the chairs in a circle, facing outward. Play music while the students walk in a circle around the chairs, and when the music stops, each student must be in a chair (multiple students per chair is okay) with his or her feet off the floor. Any student who touches the floor is out.

The next round, remove one chair and continue as before. Continue each round until only one chair is left. Use a strong chair (preferably steel reinforced) for the final round.

Hold The Spit!

Gather Alka-Seltzer tablets and water. Line up five or six volunteers at a time, giving each one a Dixie cup and a tablet. They load their mouth with water, then, after a count-down, drop a tablet into their mouth. The tablet immediately foams, filling their mouth with suds.

Time them. The longest time wins. Video recording with the slow motion feature is just… wonderful.

Floor Pong

Each player has a table tennis (ping pong) paddle and counts off in order: "One… two… three…". The net is removed from a table tennis table, and players stand around the table. Must be played on a hard floor. The #1 player serves the ball, dropping it on the floor to bounce it, and hitting it onto the TOP of the table surface. The ball bounces or rolls on the surface until it falls off. The ball MUST bounce ONE time, and then the #2 player hits it back on TOP of the table surface, until the process is repeated in the order of the players' assigned numbers.

When someone misses the table or the ball bounces on the floor twice, that person is OUT. The order of players continues as before. Example: The #3 player misses the ball and is out, so the #4 player is now hitting it AFTER the #2 player.

Round Robin Table Tennis

All players circle around a regular table tennis table. There are 2 paddles only. One person SERVES the ball (standard table tennis serve) and SETS his paddle down onto the table, then gets in the NEXT line (clockwise). The player BEHIND him in line picks up the paddle he just set down.

The other player RETURNS the ball, sets his paddle down on the table, and gets in the next line (clockwise). The player following him picks up the paddle and continues the rally, hitting it once, setting the paddle down and getting in the next line.

Play continues until a player messes up, at which point he is eliminated. Standard table tennis rules apply—it must bounce only once on your side, you must hit it over the net to the other side, it must hit the other side of the table, you must use the paddle (not your hand), if it tips the net and goes over, it is fair, etc.

Game of Letters

Divide into two teams. Each person holds one letter (listed below) printed on one sheet of paper (some people can hold two letters, if needed).

Call a word, and students run up and spell it out. The first team done scores a point.

To add a twist, insert three more letters late in the game.

Sample words:

- ENTMPASROG: Rats, smart, gore, set, master, roast, smear, togas, snore, ten proms, get spam, great son
- Add letters B-I-L: Bails, boring, lent, lamps, lips, boils great, strong meal

Do You Love Your Neighbor?

Arrange teens in a circle of chairs, facing inward. One person is in the middle.

The middle person asks any seated person, "Do you love your neighbor?"

If "No," the people on either side (the neighbors) switch seats. The middle man tries to steal an empty seat.

If "Yes," the seated person has to come up with someone he or she *does not* like. For example, he may say, "Yes, but I don't like people wearing red." Or, "Yes, but I don't like people with long hair." Every person meeting that criteria jumps up and switches seats.

The middle person tries to find an empty seat in the mayhem. Game continues indefinitely.

Death Ball

Arrange the chairs in a circle, facing inward. One person is in the middle.

Pass a beach ball from person to person without the middle man intercepting the ball. If the middle man gets the ball, the LAST PERSON to TOUCH the ball is in the middle. For example, if the ball is thrown across the room and no one catches it, the thrower has to race across the room to get his own ball before the middle man gets it. Or, if someone bounces the ball off their neighbor's knee and into the middle man's hand, the last one to touch it is in the middle.

The newest person to take a seat starts with the ball.

The ball must be SERVED to someone at least 3 chairs away (rule only applies to the serve).

The person in the middle can take a seat when:

- He intercepts the ball (last person to touch it is in the middle), OR
- He tags the person with the ball

Number Groups

Call a number, and your group has to sit down, linking arms in groups of that number. Anyone not in a group is eliminated.

Example: You have a group of 20 people, and you call, "THREE!" They grab each other and sit in groups of three (6 groups x 3 people = 18 people), so 2 people are eliminated.

Non-Active Small Assembly Games
(10-40 People)

Sword Drills

Teens raise their Bibles in the air while the leader names a Bible reference and says, "GO!" The first person to stand and point at the correct passage wins.

9-Square Tic Tac Toe

Arrange nine tic tac toe games in a 3x3 grid. Sword drills or Bible trivia lets the winner enter an X or O into *any* square. Teams must complete an entire small game in order to gain a mark toward the larger grid game.

Mafia

Preselect roles for each person, either by assigning them paper drawn from a hat or by naming the role and tapping them on the head when their eyes are closed. Each "night," your whole "town" (your group) goes to "sleep" (closes their eyes), and each "morning" they wake up to find a townsperson has been wiped out by the mafia.

Each round progresses as follows:

- Town goes to sleep.
- MAFIA members wake up (about 10% of the crowd. If 30 students, choose 3 mafia members). MAFIA quietly choose a person to eliminate, agreeing within 20 seconds.
- MAFIA goes to sleep.

- DOCTOR wakes up and chooses to HEAL someone by pointing at one student (can choose himself). If the MAFIA had targeted that person, the doctor would heal him and he would NOT be eliminated.
- DOCTOR goes to sleep.
- POLICE MAN wakes up. He points at a person and the moderator nods YES if that person is MAFIA, or shakes his head NO if that person is a townsperson.
- POLICE goes to sleep.
- Town wakes up, and the moderator indicates what happened (make up a story of the MAFIA sneaking into town and eliminating a townsperson).
- If the DOCTOR did not choose to HEAL that person, that person is eliminated and can no longer speak, but can observe the game.
- Then, the town VOTES by majority to eliminate someone from the game, trying to weed out the MAFIA from their midst. They are given a set time to deliberate and nominate (say, 2 minutes) and then VOTE by raised hands. If the nominee receives a majority vote, he is eliminated from the game.
    - Note: Anyone can claim anything they want. "I'm the police man! And I asked if HE is mafia, and he is! I'm serious, guys!" Or, "No way, I'm not mafia! I heard JOE moving around. I think HE is mafia! Let's vote HIM out!"
    - I prefer keeping the roles secret, even after the person is eliminated. At the end of each round, indicate whether there are still mafia or not, and continue to the next.

Rounds continue until:
- All the townspeople are eliminated (MAFIA wins), OR
- All the mafia are eliminated (TOWNSPEOPLE win)

Contact

The Word Master secretly writes a word down and hides it in his pocket (i.e. INFLATIONARY). He writes the first letter on the board. ("I")

Any student submits a one-word clue relating to that letter (i.e. "Country"), and, if another student thinks he knows the word that the clue is referring to, he'll say, "CONTACT."

The Word Master has one chance to guess what word the clue referred to ("Is it… Indonesia?").

If he is wrong, he gives a "3-2-1" countdown to the two CONTACT students, who simultaneously say their guess out loud ("India!"). If their words match each other, they win that round and the Game Master must add another letter to reveal his word ("I-N"). If the two CONTACT students did not say the same word simultaneously, another clue is given by someone else.

Play continues until the students can GUESS the Word Master's word. It must be an exact match, and the players can only submit THREE guesses over the course of the game. Example: if the board said "I-N-F-L-A-T-I-," a guess of *INFLATION* would be incorrect (since the word is *inflationary*), and play would continue with TWO guesses remaining.

Boppity Bop Bop Bop

The leader stands in the middle of the circle, points at someone who is seated and says, "Boppity Bop Bop Bop." Before the leader finishes his "Boppity Bop Bop Bop," the seated person must say "Bop," or else he takes the leader role in the middle of the circle.

Once participants become proficient at this, other tasks can be added (i.e. Elephant 1, 2, 3; Kamikaze 1, 2, 3). In addition to "Boppity Bop Bop Bop," the leader has the option of saying any of those commands.

If the leader says, "Elephant 1, 2, 3" to you, you must stack both fists on your nose like an elephant trunk. The person to your left and right must use his arm to make an elephant ear on his head giving respect to which side of the nose he is on (i.e. if on the right side, he's the right ear). The slowest person to complete his task becomes the new leader in the center of the circle.

If the leader says, "Kamikaze 1, 2, 3" to you, you must put your hands up to your eyes in circles to make flight goggles. The person to your left and right must stick his arm straight out like an airplane wing giving respect to which side of the pilot he is on (i.e. if on the right side, he's the right wing). Again, the slowest person to complete the task becomes the new leader.

Big Bang

Chairs are in a circle, with a person in the middle as the SHOOTER.

The **SHOOTER** points to a person in the circle (**VICTIM**) and "shoots" his sign (progression: 1. bang, 2. bang-bang, 3. boom, then 4. boom-boom.)

The **victim** DUCKS under the shot.

The people on either side of the victim (**BYSTANDERS**) SHOOT EACH OTHER with a "hand" gun and their sign (whatever stage of the progression they're on.)

The LAST person to react goes to the middle as the new **shooter**. OR, the person who MESSES UP their sign goes to the middle (i.e. if someone was supposed to say #2 "Bang-bang" but they instead shouted #3 "Boom!")

*Example: JOHN is in the middle as the **shooter**, and John has already messed up once, so he is on Stage 2 in the progression ("Bang-bang.")*

*JOHN points to SUZIE (**victim**) and yells, "Bang-bang."*

SUZIE ducks to avoid the shot.

*Sitting on either side of SUZIE (**victim**) are ROBERT and SARAH (**bystanders**).*

*ROBERT (**bystander**) points at SARAH (**bystander**) and shoots her with "Bang."*

*SARAH (**bystander**) points at ROBERT (**bystander**) and shoots him with "Bang."*

ROBERT shot SARAH first, so SARAH moves to the middle and is now on #2: "Bang-bang." And JOHN takes her seat.

*Now, SARAH (**new shooter**) points to JOHN (**new victim**) and says, "Bang-bang."*

Play continues as long as you would like (i.e. until someone is out, until everyone is out, for 10 minutes, until no one is left on Stage 1, etc.)

Signs

Chairs are in a circle, facing inward, with one person in the middle. Each student (ideal group size is less than 20) chooses a "sign" such as scratching their beard, pulling an ear, raising a hand, flipping their hair, or flapping a chicken wing. The "sign" is secretly SENT from one person and RECEIVED by the other person (the round starts with the middle person's eyes closed, but other signs are sent with the middle person trying to catch the passing).

- SEND a sign – do another person's sign, i.e. "scratch the beard."
- RECEIVE a sign – do YOUR sign, indicating you saw it passed and you received it. Example: if you are the ear-puller and someone SENDS your sign by pulling their ear, you pull your ear to RECEIVE the sign.

If the person in the middle sees the signs being sent or received (or if he has probable cause), he asks someone, "Do YOU have it?" If yes, that person is in the middle. If not, play continues as before.

Head Moose

Circle the chairs, facing inward. Each CHAIR receives an animal "sign."

The first chair is the "Head Moose," and the order of chairs goes clockwise. The Head Moose's sign is moose antlers (2 open hands, palms out, thumbs on temples.)

The other chairs choose signs. They can be anything you can think of that can easily be seen by everyone in the circle. Some examples:

- Snake – hand "slithers" in an "s" shape away from your body
- Raccoon – two circles over the eyes
- Shark – "fin" hand on top of head
- Rabbit – 2 finger "bunny ears" behind head
- Bear – 2 claws raised
- Tiger – 1 claw swiped diagonally

PLAY:

- The Head Moose always starts.
- He begins with HIS OWN sign (moose antlers.)
- He then does SOMEONE ELSE'S sign, "sending" it to them. (e.g. the bunny ears)
- The person in the RABBIT chair does HIS OWN rabbit sign (bunny ears) to "receive" the sign.
- Then the rabbit does SOMEONE ELSE'S sign to pass it off again (e.g. the "snake" sign). He can pass it to anyone, including the person who just sent it.

Play continues until someone fails. You fail by:

- "Receiving" your sign incorrectly (e.g. doing the wrong sign)
- Hesitating too long
- Moving out of turn (e.g. the sign is passed to the "bear" but the "tiger" person moves. The "tiger" would fail.)

Once someone FAILS, he goes to the LAST CHAIR (to the right of the "Head Moose.")

Everyone that was behind him in line then SHIFTS UP one chair.

The sign is assigned to the CHAIR and NOT the PERSON. Everyone who shifted chairs gets the new sign associated with the chair.

Play continues indefinitely. The goal is to become the Head Moose.

PSST

Arrange the teens in a circle. One person starts by cupping the side of his mouth with either the right or left hand.

If he cups the right side of his mouth with his right hand, the "psst" is passed to the person to his left. If he cups the left side of his mouth with his left hand, it is passed right.

The person to whom the "psst" is passed must immediately pass it back or pass it on (right or left hand). If he hesitates, he fails.

Contestants progress through FIVE STAGES as they fail:

- Psst
- Psst, psst
- Ding
- Dong
- PACKAW!

Failures happen 3 ways:

- They hesitate when it is passed to them
- They do the wrong stage
- They move when it is not passed to them

Once a person fails on "PACKAW!," he or she is officially out.

The final round between two people progresses through all 5 stages and repeats until someone messes up. They can use either hand to pass it on.

Couch (Also called "Four On the Couch")

Chairs are in a circle, facing inward, with one open seat. Split the teams evenly (i.e. guys/girls) and write each person's name on a piece of paper.

Four chairs serve as the COUCH. The rest of the chairs are PAIRED as units (chairs 1-2 are a pair, chairs 3-4 are a pair, etc.) One PAIR of chairs will have the open seat.

Students secretly pull names from a hat, and they "become" the name on their paper. Whoever has the open seat beside him calls a random name. Whoever has THAT name (the one that was called) on their PAPER will move to the open seat, and the PAIR will SWITCH PAPERS (the person who called the name now "becomes" that person).

Example:

- JOHN (has "George" name on paper) calls for "Suzie."
- WILBUR has the "Suzie" paper, so WILBUR ("Suzie") moves to the open seat beside JOHN ("George") and they switch papers.
- Now, JOHN becomes "Suzie" and WILBUR becomes "George."
- The group knows JOHN's name (because he just called "Suzie"), but they do not know WILBUR's name (because he secretly traded to become "George," which had not been called yet).

Play continues until those on the COUCH are removed and replaced by four teammates. For example, if the teams are guys vs. girls, if four guy bodies are sitting on the COUCH (regardless of their "names"), the guys win.

Up Front Games (Large Assembly)

Total Blackout

Source. We saw clips of a show on hulu.com called "Total Blackout" that sparked the idea for this game. *(Disclaimer: while they *bleep out the curse words, this is not a clean show. We do not recommend nor regularly watch the show.)* Contestants are placed into a dark room and told to do a variety of things: identify objects, race through a maze, guess the weight, etc. Sometimes, for example, they are feeling a camel or a crocodile and trying to guess the weight. Sometimes, they have a glass globe put around their head and they can only guess the item based on feeling it on their face. This is all while completely blind and scared.

Adaptation. We adapted the show with a blindfold, 4 contestants and 5 tubs. In each tub was an item they had to identify while blindfolded.

We wanted it to be as scary and gross as possible.

PREPARATION:

- Two people from each team (4 people total)
- Blindfold – swimming goggles spray-painted so you cannot see through
- Table
- Items in place
- Timer
- Score keeper

EXPLAIN TO CONTESTANTS:

Uncover BOXED items (lids on so you don't see and so they don't get away), you'll have to guess what they are by feel. Some, use your HAND. Some, use only your FACE.

TIMED event – As many as you complete in 3 minutes OR the fastest time for all 4 or 5 items.

PERSON 1 (from each team)	PERSON 2 (from each team)
Goldfish live – use hand	Ramen – use hand
Raisins – use hand	Mustard – use hand
Grass – use face	Pine cone – use face
Wig – use face	Teddy bear – use face
Other ideas – popcorn, costume hand, etc.	Smelly work shoe – use face

2014 Preaching Rally:

ROUND 1	ROUND 2 (identify flavored soda)	ROUND 3	ROUND 4
Sponge/toothpicks	Coffee	Live goldfish	Raisins
Mustard (prep baby wipes)	Peanut butter	Diaper (with old browned banana)	Lizard (15" hissing lizard!)
Fuzzy hat	Ranch	Jell-O	Tape donut
Wig	Sweet corn	Pine cone	Shoe (nasty work shoe)
Spikey ball	Bacon	Pool balls	Grass (decorative plant)
Ideas: mouse trap, rope	Buffalo sauce		

Games | 43

Outdoor Games

Ninja

Standing in a circle, each person has ONE movement to try to touch someone else's hand (i.e. lunge at someone or slap at their hand), but is then frozen in place. The defender has ONE movement to get away, and is also frozen in the new position.

Play continues around the circle with each person receiving ONE movement and immediately the next person takes his ONE movement (each time, the defender can dodge an attack). If someone's hand is touched, that HAND is out (put behind their back), but their other HAND is still in. Once BOTH hands are eliminated, that PERSON is out of the game.

One-Pitch Softball

Split the teams evenly. Regular softball rules apply for running the bags, fielding, etc.

Teams choose their own pitcher. Each player on the team gets ONE pitch, and the entire team bats through their rotation.

The pitcher has FIVE SECONDS from the end of the play to pitch the next ball. Umpire counts down audibly.

If the runner is tagged, forced out, or a fly ball is caught, the runner is out and play continues to the next batter.

Runs are tallied through each inning.

Rounds is over after the last batter hits. Umpire begins TEN SECOND countdown as teams switch fields. Pitcher MUST pitch his first pitch BEFORE the 10s countdown ends.

This works with outdoor softball and indoor kickball. It is fast-paced and is a great way to involve ALL the teens of the group, no matter their skill level.

Outpost

We adapted this game from the book *Adventure Games* by Jeff Hopper, Steve Torrey and Rod Yonkers.

SETUP. Divide into two teams, giving each player a strip of colored caution tape or football flags for pulling and identifying their team. After the rules are discussed as a group, teams meet separately for eight minutes to assign their roles and strategize their playtime. Teams wait near their starting places outdoors until the starting siren.

The following is the handout we gave to every player:

OBJECT. Players earn points in 3 ways:

- Capture enemy generals
- Capture enemy players
- Scouts tag Field Marshal for information

UNPC. The United Nations Peace Central is a centrally located spot where rules are given, quarrels are resolved, captured players are turned in, and points are distributed.

FLAGS. Flags are worn by everyone in their back pockets. The flags must be able to be pulled freely from the pocket. At least one half of the flag must be hanging outside of the pocket to be visible.

CAPTURING THE ENEMY. Soldiers are captured and become prisoners when their flag is pulled form their pocket by an enemy. Physical force may not be used in trying to pull a flag. Players may not hold, sit on, or lean against anything when trying to defend their flags.

Once a capture has been made:

- All action stops for both players
- Neither player may capture or be captured
- The prisoner is escorted by the capturing player to the UNPC for points, or the capturing player may elect to set the prisoner free. All prisoners must be escorted by the capturing player, with one exception—generals may give captured prisoners to other players to be escorted back.

Field marshals can neither capture nor be captured.

LIVES. All soldiers start with a designated number of lives according to their rank. A life is taken away every time a soldier is captured. When players run out of lives, they become scouts.

SCOUTS. Scouts can neither capture nor be captured. Scouts play an important role in obtaining enemy information and locations.

Scouts may tag Field Marshals in the back for information cards. These are turned in at UNPC for 1,000 points each.

Only scouts may try to unscramble the secret message (Bible verse) formed by the information cards. The first team to figure out the secret message receives 15,000 points.

There are NO time-outs!

END. The game ends when all 5 generals are captured OR when the leaders decide.

CHARACTERS

RANK	LIVES	POINTS
General	1	20,000+
Lieutenant	2	10,000
Sergeant	3	5,000
Infantry	3	1,000
Scout	0	0
Field Marshal	NA	0

Time Killers

My teens get bored easily. We use these games to pass the time on bus rides or in line at amusement parks.

My Fishy

Simply say, "Um… My fishy likes your shirt… Um… my fishy likes the sky… Um… my fishy likes to eat pork." See if they start catching on. The catch is, all you have to do is begin each "my fishy likes" with "Um." When the teens guess, they'll say, "Well, my fishy likes black hair." To which you'll reply, "Nope. Um… my fishy likes to play this game." They'll try to figure everything from the alphabet to the color of the items you're guessing about.

Throw the Ball

Say, "I throw the ball to John, he throws the ball to Sam, Sam throws the ball to Cassi, she throws it to me, and I throw it to Mrs. Jamie. Who has the ball?" The first person to talk has the ball. They'll try to look for all kinds of alphabet clues and other funny connections.

I'm Going On Vacation

Say, "I'm going on vacation and I'm going to take a Rolls Royce. What are you going to take?" My initials are RR (Ryan Rench), so I will take two items beginning with *R*. John Smith might take a Juniper tree and a Sucker.

Johnny Whoop!

Hold your left hand up, and with your right index finger, point to each finger and say "Johnny." At the index finger, "slide" down to the thumb saying "Whoop!" then repeat in reverse order. For example, the sequence is "Johnny, Johnny, Johnny, Johnny, Whoop! Johnny, Whoop! Johnny, Johnny, Johnny, Johnny." The "Secret Key" can be anything done before or after to get it "right": you can start the sequence by saying, "Watch carefully," or end the sequence by folding the hands or saying, "Now you try." The people who do not do the "Secret Key" will be stumped until they pick up on the repeated clues.

9+6=3

Use a clock face to do "simple" adding and subtracting. NINE (o' clock) plus SIX (hours) equals THREE (o' clock). Hence, 2-4=10, and 8+11=7. Once they catch on to the secret, add a twist by counting the minutes instead of hours. Example: 105 (1:05) minus 60 (minutes) equals 1,205 (12:05).

Around the World

Each person says a location that they will go next in a sequence A-R-O-U-N-D the world (first letter). For example: A-ugusta, R-aleigh, O-hio, U-tah, N-evada, D-enmark, A-msterdam, etc.

Where Are You Going Next?

Each person says a location they will go next in a sequence, starting with a letter of the last letter of the previous word. For example, one person says, "I'm going to CALIFORNIA," and the next person says a place starting with *A*, such as, "I'm going to Alabama." The next person's place also starts with *A*, such as "I'm going to Arkansas," and the next will say, "Savannah."

Green Glass Door

Say something like, "Behind the green glass door are BOOTS but not SHOES," or, "Behind the green glass door are SCHOOLS but not STUDENTS." The trick is that the first word has a double-letter, and the second does not.

This Is a Pen

Say, "OK, this is a pen, this is a pen, this is a pen, and this is a pen." Each time, hold the pen in a different hand or facing a different direction, thus misleading the others. Then hold up the pen and ask, "Is THIS a pen?" The trick is that it IS a pen IF you started your sequence with the word OK. If you did not say, "OK..." then it is NOT a pen.

Twenty Sick Sheep

Say, "A man has 20 sick sheep. One dies. How many are left?" The phrase "twenty sick sheep" sounds like "twenty-six sheep" and it will leave them guessing for a while.

Wednesday

"A cowboy rides into town on Wednesday, stays for *3 days*, and rides out of town *again* on Wednesday. How is this possible?" The horse's name is Wednesday.

Coffin

"The guy who bought it does not want it. The guy who built it does not need it. The guy who's using it does not know he's using it. What is it?" A coffin.

Hole

"What can you put in a barrel that is weightless, you can see it with the naked eye, and when it is added, it makes the barrel lighter?" A hole.

5. Fundraisers

Comedy Night

Each summer, our teens learn skits and host a 45-minute show for the church. We sell tickets at $5 each, or $25 per family, which includes a light meal before the show (nachos, potato bar, etc.). We sell additional goods (1 dozen frozen lumpia, premium baked goods, etc.) for additional funds.

We prepare months in advance, gathering skits and scripts from January through April, then practice weekly from April through June. Our event is just before camp in July, and we rehearse on Wednesday nights in lieu of our 25-minute game time.

We work to make each skit as entertaining as possible, and include props, well-rehearsed lines, video skits, background music and anything else that will make the night run as smoothly as possible.

I have hundreds of scripts on file, and can share them with you, if you are interested in doing something similar. After discovering a clean comedy sketch group called Studio C on YouTube, we use their content almost exclusively.

The latest scripts that I have from Studio C are listed below:

- We Need an Answer, Mr. President
- Substitute Teacher Problems
- The Real Death Clock
- Longest Checkout Line

- Bop It Extreme
- Wonder Woman Fights for Justice League Equality
- Easily Offended Friends
- Doctor Refuses to Help Man
- Political Correctness Puzzles Police
- That Baby Be Ugly
- Mean Girls
- The Real Bully
- Hazel – Most Annoying Coworker
- Plane Crash
- Shooting Gallery
- Two Truths and a Lie
- Judge Not
- Bad Extra
- Who Wants to Be a Millionaire
- Is This Yours
- Most Accurate Mood Ring
- Marco Polo
- Super Sibling
- Naturally
- Weighty Matters
- Prop Switch
- Foreign Exchange
- Dead Wedding
- Scary Stories from the Future

The fundraiser raises about $500 and is split among the attendees who are going to camp.

Yard Sale

For four weeks, our church collects donations from church members to use in our annual yard sale. We store items in an unused classroom for three weeks, then in the final week before the sale, we use teen work days to stage the items on various tables by category.

Large items are listed on Craigslist (many sell before the Saturday sale). The Saturday yard sale lasts from 6:00 am to 12:00 pm, at which point the teens clean up and return home. The following day, items are sold to our church members for 50% off. Any remaining items are donated to a missionary in Mexico.

We have historically raised over $2,000 dollars, which is split evenly among the 20 (or so) workers according to an hourly wage (includes prep-days and yard sale day). Rather than pestering our church members for donations, this fundraiser benefits our church by raising funds from *outside* our church, AND it gives church members an opportunity to get rid of some accumulated junk.

Cookies (With Donation Bucket)

After an event like our annual Christmas program, our church is invited to our gym for fellowship time. Rather than selling items (overpriced bake sale, anyone?), the teens provide baked cookies and serve during the fellowship time. The only funds raised are from a donation bucket stationed at the front door. Every teen who served and donated cookies is included in the donations received from that event. Everyone benefits from the food and church-wide fellowship (no one is left out if they could not afford a baked good), and a few donors give generously to support the teens.

Table Tennis Tournament

We scoured the internet and garage sales for good deals on several table tennis tables, as well as borrowed some from church members, and on a Saturday afternoon we arranged a double-elimination table tennis tournament. Contestants signed up ahead of time and paid an entry fee of $10 for adults, and $5 for the kids' bracket. All proceeds benefited the youth fund.

6. Various Youth Ideas

Youth Philosophy

The following article was printed in the May edition of the Global Baptist Times, a publication of the Global Independent Baptist Fellowship:

Philosophy, Meet Practicality

Because of the God-ordained structure in families, any good youth ministry will operate under the parents' authority at all times. The main responsibility of the teens' spiritual lives rests on their parents, not the youth pastor, and the *philosophy* of our youth ministry is that children are given to parents.

Practically speaking, however, most of our *time* is spent with the teens, not the families. We do everything possible to spiritually influence the teens individually, mainly by highlighting the Bible's importance in their lives. We believe that when a teen truly sees the Bible as supreme, everyone is helped. Weekly expository Bible preaching (rather than a curriculum) geared and applied directly for them, weekly how-to Bible study classes and weekly articles and notes help drive this point home, and we deliberately view every time we interact with them as a chance to see them helped spiritually.

Some see the youth Sunday school and midweek Bible study as a threat to family time. I say, two hours a week is a threat?! With the correct focus of both church and family, we cannot help but think that a Bible-based youth ministry can *only* help everyone involved.

Preaching Rally

Overview: The Preaching Rally is a one-day youth conference centered on one theme.

Explanation: The Preaching Rally is based on the model set by the Men's Advance, a national men's meeting hosted by Bible Baptist Church in Stillwater, OK. While the Men's Advance is a two-day event and the Preaching Rally is only one day, the concept is the same. The decorations, printed materials, promotional materials, music, skits and especially the preaching is centered on one theme, each building on the previous.

The Preaching Rally is a 4.5-hour youth rally with three preaching sessions focused on one theme. Each aspect of the Preaching Rally drives home this one idea so that the whole event is like one sermon with three main points.

Reasoning: Some of the reasoning behind hosting the Preaching Rally is to promote fellowship among area churches and provide an environment in which God can speak through the preaching of His Word. Games, skits and food all add to the enjoyment of the day, but the impact of the Preaching Rally comes through the directed preaching sessions.

God speaks today primarily through His Word, and limiting the preachers to a specific direction in no way limits God's speaking as long as the preached message is what God says in the Bible. By directing the topics of each preaching session and all the various aspects of the Preaching Rally, the overall impact of the Preaching Rally does not come from a "big-name" preacher but from the content. *Content* drives everything, and we believe this model is self-sustaining and enduring.

Further, excellence is key in presenting the Preaching Rally. Our desire is to simply provide an impactful day in which God can speak free of distractions, so we want every video to be perfect, every skit to be flawless, every meal to be efficient and every detail to flow smoothly. It is not always perfect, but the goal is not perfection… the goal is to not be noticed. A proper view of excellence has others in mind before self, and simple oversight or lack of preparation often distracts from many services.

Timeline/Schedule:

Preparation

- 6 months   Save the date postcard
- 2 months   Intro letter sent
- 1 month   Promo Packet sent
- 1 week   Complete all prep

Preaching Rally

- 10:30   Free group photos
- **11:00   Sess. 1 – Opening Video/songs**
- 11:10   Giveaways/games
- 11:20   Skit/songs
- 11:30   Special Music
- 11:35   Preaching
- 12:15   Break
- **12:25   Sess. 2 – Skit/songs/special**
- 12:40   Preaching
- 1:30   Lunch
- **2:05   Sess. 3 – Songs/games**
- 2:20   Skit/songs/special music
- 2:35   Preaching
- 3:15   Invitation/closing
- 3:30   Dismissal

Following

- 1 Month after – Follow-up postcard/website updates announcement

Breakdown: Many different aspects/areas go into the Preaching Rally. Each area has a designated "chief" that reports in as often as necessary (per their area), and the PR overseer's job is to train and equip the chiefs as best as possible. The areas are as follows:

- **Graphics.** The first impact of the Preaching Rally will come through the graphics. By the time the teens get to the Preaching Rally they'll have already been exposed to the idea of the day through the printed and online materials.
    - **Mailings.** First, several mailings are sent to each church on our area churches list (about 200):
        - **6 months.** Save the date postcard.
        - **2 months.** Intro letter sent. Explains the PR and mentions Promo Packet coming. Includes a letter from the host pastor and youth pastor on themed letterhead.
        - **1 month.** Promo Packet sent. Includes 11x17 posters, letter of explanation, announcement sheet templates, postcard templates, and signup sheets.
        - **1 month after.** Follow-up postcard. Mentions updates to the website preachingrally.com including pictures, videos and next year's information.
    - **Banner.** A themed banner is posted at church one month prior to get the church involved and to welcome the guests upon arrival.
    - **Preaching Rally graphics.** Several printed materials are given to each attendee:
        - **Booklet.** Includes notes, theme explanation, welcome, next year's information, schedules, maps, and more.
        - **Pen.** Themed.
        - **Gift bag.** On their way out, they receive a bag of candy with themed scratch paper and a bookmark.

- o **Youth pastor welcome.** All youth pastors and pastors who come receive a personal letter from the host and a special booklet of information explaining the day.

- o **"The Review."** The following Sunday at church, the members get to see dozens of pictures printed and read a review of the day. This is encouraging and exciting.

- **Decorations.** Another big area of the Preaching Rally are the decorations. Since we desire everything to add impact and emphasize the message, the decorations play a huge part. The whole platform is set with major backdrops, and the interior walls are lined with more decorations. The exterior of the building is decorated as well so that as they walk up the steps they are immersed in the message. The Decorating Chief sets up her own teams and meeting times on her own, but all the decorations ideas based on approval by the PR overseer. Several months are needed to plan the direction and the execution of the decorations.

- **Registration.** All based on our mailing spreadsheet, the Registration Chief coordinates the pre-registration, anticipates the attendance, gathers and updates all the necessary information on the churches and youth pastors, coordinates mailings and assembles the registration team the day of the PR.

- **Hospitality.** Working closely with the registration team, the greeters are the first ones to welcome the PR attendees. The Chief places her team of volunteers all over the church property so that every attendee is greeted, handed a booklet and pen, and is directed to a seat. Also, each main greeter is given a list and pictures of the youth pastors so that they can greet them and their church by name.

- **Parking attendants.** Also working closely with the greeters, the parking attendants make sure the buses are parked properly and efficiently so that every attendee knows where to go. The Chief coordinates drop-off locations and his attendants and instructs them on how to direct, greet and where to stand.

- **Skits.** A couple months of preparation goes into the skits which are written by the chief and tied to the theme. He chooses his actors and plans practice times, props, sound checks and all other details accordingly. The skits are not long and they are funny, working to find the balance between getting a point across while still being a skit. MUCH humor is used.

- **Photography.** Several professional photographers attend our church and are used for preparation and for the day of the PR. They filter through their pictures the night of the PR and present about 50 to be printed and posted on the website asap. The rest of their photos come out the following week.

- **Video.** Several videos are made each year for the PR, including a promotional video and an intro video. Further, countdown videos are used to gain attention and settle the audience during the PR.

- **Website.** Everything possible is posted on the website as soon as possible. All graphics, backgrounds, mailings, promotional materials and information is posted on the website in order to assist the youth pastors in promoting the PR within their group.

- **Food.** We charge $5 per attendee to cover the cost of the food and other expenses, and provide them a full pizza meal with sodas and waters. The speed of service is analyzed each year and we try to get as many through the lines as quickly as possible.

- **Maintenance/Grounds.** Even something small might be a distraction, and in preparation we want to make the grounds as presentable as possible. Several weeks of small preparations and one large full-church workday gets the grounds looking very nice for our guests.

- **Assembly Teams.** Several different assembly teams are used throughout the process including one for each mailing and for the gift bags.

- **Cleaning.** The Cleaning Chief designates areas to oversee and does a full cleaning after the Preaching Rally.

- **Sound.** Sound-checks are scheduled and approved through the PR overseer, and a full run-through practice is done the night before the PR.

- **Songs.** The song-leader chooses and has the songs approved by the PR overseer and gets the wording to the Media Chief.

- **Media.** This Chief is to oversee all video presentations and PowerPoint displays including pictures, backdrops, sermon media, lyrics and more.

- **Nursery.** This Chief coordinates nursery and childcare for the PR.

- **Guest Preachers.** The PR overseer (host youth pastor) communicates with the guest preachers more than a year in advance. He schedules the preachers, communicates the goal of the PR, discusses the theme, and answers any questions. Throughout the preparation process he checks in with the guest preachers to make sure the direction of their sessions goes the same direction as the whole Preaching Rally, and he makes adjustments where necessary.

Past Preaching Rally Themes:

I choose themes based on important topics among teens. I think, "What would have helped ME as a teen, and what resonates with my teens?" Here are the themes and graphics that we have used over the past few years:

Surrender. Brother Bryan Samms preached powerful messages on the topic of surrender. The exterior and interior decorations depicted the battleship where the document of unconditional surrender was signed as Japan yielded to the Allied Forces of World War II. The graphics depicted the raised hands of surrender.

Choose to Abound. Pastor Jason Gaddis and Pastor Wayne Hardy preached pointed messages on God's abundant blessings from the story of God's provision for Ruth. The tagline of the theme was, "Healthy waters produce abundant living," challenging Christians to obey God and enjoy his abundance. The exterior decorations showed the filth and trash of OUR way (unhealthy waters), while the interior decorations took us underwater to teeming fish and abundant coral — life HIS way (healthy waters)!

Timeless. With the onslaught of trendy and new, Christian teens need to be anchored to something that will not change. The Israelites had their monuments, as in the days of Joshua. Brother John Lande challenged teens to choose the timeless over the trendy, while the decorations transported us to the scene where Joshua crossed the Jordan River and set up 12 stones for future generations. Concluding the meeting, attendees were given a 150-page book on the theme called *A Case for Being Timeless*, available in paperback and audiobook from Calvary Baptist Publications on Amazon.com.

Pure Love. Pastor David Hetzer preached powerful sermons on purity and marriage—God's commands for future spouses. The decorations took us to an ice cream parlor as we were challenged to build "Ice Cream Sundae Relationships," and the skits, music, and even the ice cream sundae snack made the point clear. As attendees were dismissed, they received the minibook, *A Case for Being Timeless* (kindle and audiobook available on Amazon.com) and a brochure that visually explained the "Ice Cream Sundae Relationships."

Gender Matters. In the same year that Facebook unveiled about 43 different gender options, President Obama openly defended homosexuality and Apple CEO Tim Cook came out as gay, our church hosted the Preaching Rally on the theme "Gender Matters." Bro. Rick and Mrs. Anna Williams preached and taught on the theme, using two combined sessions and one split session (men and ladies) to show the importance of following God's direction when it comes to our gender. The graphics were the stereotypical pink/blue contrast, and all the games and decorations added to the theme.

Do Something. David's mighty men visited our church through the preaching of Michael Jones, challenging the teens to Do Something Special, Do Something Strong, and Do Something Selfless. The walls were covered with swords, spears and shields, and the platform was the scene of the Philistine camp where David's mighty men got David some water from his favorite well. The graphics were rugged and fierce, emphasizing the need for strength in the Christian walk.

The PREACHING RALLY. For a detailed book covering every aspect of the Preaching Rally as outlined above, please see the book review of *The PREACHING RALLY: How to plan and run a one-day youth conference* in Chapter 7 – Books.

Youth Nights

Once per month, our teens are in the main service to serve through singing, ushering and song-leading. I am training a new teen each month to lead the singing, and the guys are serving through ushering and greeting.

In addition, one of our pianists will usually play the offertory and a teen will provide the special music for the evening. This is a great way to get teens involved in ministry and in ministry training. It gives them good experience and opportunities to serve.

It takes the place of our game time. After the song service in the main sanctuary, we then immediately go up to our room for the sermon.

I tried to anticipate complaints and head them off through teaching. I taught and preached on serving the Lord, I wrote articles on how they should react when the time came, and I tried to give announcements that would train them even how to think about the others who are involved in the music.

Since we were intentional about it, the teens responded well and enjoyed the service. They did not miss their game time at all!

Our monthly youth nights strengthen our young people. Whether they realize it or not, they are gaining valuable experience in the public service that they are involved in. By ushering, praying in front of the church, leading the congregational singing, doing the special music and greeting people before services, they are stretching themselves beyond what a lot of adults are willing to do! I have loved our youth nights and we will continue doing them.

Announcement Sheets

Explanation: Every class (Sunday school and Wednesday night) we have teen greeters in place to hand out our weekly announcement sheets. These include any announcement within two weeks on our calendar, songs, and a note from me. Sometimes the note is silly, sometimes it is instructional, sometimes it is long, and sometimes short.

At times I will expand the announcement sheet to include something from the lesson that day, or I will include a general handout. This helps save time in class because I am not wasting time handing out information.

The weekly announcement sheets foster an expectation and help immensely on communication. I rarely get asked details about an activity because they're always on the announcement sheets.

Process: I update the announcement sheets on Tuesday mornings, save them in Dropbox and the secretary prints on Sunday mornings. Usually I will include some details or a funny thing that happened that week. After Sunday, a teen volunteer who is also shared on the Dropbox folder posts the information to our church website. This way the parents have access as well.

Reception: I LOVE the announcement sheets. It is one of the most important but probably most-overlooked area because it has become routine. I am okay with that.

Writing is one way to communicate love. It is also another "voice" in order to correct, get specific, get direct, or be funny. It is a simple way to share a dumb picture or a story or… whatever! The teens have come to expect and appreciate them.

One Youth Pastor's Toolbox

HOW AM I DOING?

On a scale of 1-10 (10 being the best), rate yourself like God would rate you in the following areas:

AREA	AT THE YWR	TODAY?
Missions (passion)	—	—
Tithe	—	—
Missions (giving)	—	—
TOF Home Missions Fund	—	—
Bus Ministry (passion, prayer)	—	—
Camp Decisions	—	—
Door-knocking/Saturation	—	—
Soul-winning	—	—
Spirit (attitude, respect)	—	—
Loving God	—	—
Loving others	—	—
Be Our Guest	—	—
Memorization	—	—
Service	—	—
Guest Preachers	—	—
Bible College (openness)	—	—
Mentoring/Assimilation	—	—
Church attendance	—	—
Attentiveness to Preaching	—	—
Response to Preaching	—	—
Daily Bible Reading	—	—
Daily Prayer	—	—
Altar (like #20)	—	—
Using Spiritual Gifts	—	—
Overall	—	—

You rated yourself at the Youth Winter Rendezvous. Your strengths AND your weaknesses are shown in this format, and as a Christian you always need to work on both. Keep up the good work! -Bro. Ryan

Self Report Cards

Overview: Teens rate themselves on certain spiritual disciplines that we've taught on over the past year.

Explanation: One year at our youth winter camp (Youth Winter Rendezvous), during our church's split session, I spent about 20 minutes asking the teens to rate themselves on how they had been doing on certain spiritual disciplines that I had been preaching on throughout the year. This was the first time I had done anything like this, and I went back in my mind over the past year and thought through some of the high points that I had been trying to emphasize through the preaching, asking them to rate themselves as if God were the one rating them. I read them each item audibly while they wrote their answer privately in their seats.

Results: I was pleasantly surprised at the results. Of all the sessions we had over the three days, this one was the most impactful for many of the teens. To be forced to put a number on a piece of paper as if God were doing the judging was eye-opening to some of them. Based on a scale of 1-10, 1 being pitiful and 10 being Bible-perfect, I was surprised not only at their honesty but at how few of them had been as introspective as they probably should be. It was a huge help to our group.

Follow-up: After the Rendezvous I collected their answers, read through their comments and added their answers and comments to a spreadsheet. For each teen I sorted the list from their lowest to highest answers and printed them. Over the next couple weeks, I mailed them their results and tried to encourage them with a hand-written note included.

Future Plans

Overview: Teens wrote out their 2, 5, and 10-year plans for life.

Explanation: At a recent campout activity we spent a morning around the picnic tables and I asked them to fill out their 2-year, 5-year and 10-year plans for each of the following areas: spiritual (spiritual growth, church ministry…), family (status, kids…), and life (job, location…).

After taking time to write out their goals, we discussed each area and had each person share at least one thing. I added any spiritual insight that I could to each topic that was discussed and always steered the conversation as it developed.

Results: The group discussions were very encouraging. The teens were thoughtful, intentional, and deeper than expected. Their answers had some substance to them. Some lessons that I learned were that they have dreams and goals for their lives. Often their dreams are shaped by peer pressure, and positive peer pressure and proper biblical teaching over the course of time can help steer a teen's goals in a godly direction.

Game Room

One summer, our interns tore a wall down and opened up an unused classroom that we are now using as our game room. We also redecorated the room, repainting the walls and hanging several more 8x10, 10x13, and 11x17 frames (under $5 ea. at walmart.com). We have a wall dedicated to our camp photos, a wall dedicated to our Preaching Rally posters, a wall dedicated to Bible college, a chalkboard wall and random photos from recent activities scattered everywhere else. The game room opened up a social area where we built a bar-height counter on which we place our signup sheets, brochures, picture books (all the pictures we replace in the frames go in binders), pens and more.

Our youth room is now less cramped and feels very welcoming with the new colors and pictures. Also, the pictures allow us as independent Baptists to show immediately that we are normal people with normal lives. Conservative churches do not have to portray "stuffiness" or somehow be "untouchable." Pictures of teens having fun helps accomplish that goal.

Camp T-Shirts

Each year for camp we unveil a new camp t-shirt. Our first full year as youth directors (2011), this idea helped build excitement and unity as it was a new and exciting idea. We did a simple blue shirt with our logo and class verse.

The next year (2012), we reused the logo and stylized our little mantra: "Love God, love others, do right." The maroon shirts were intentionally designed to not be too edgy so as to give a non-Christian impression, but still cool (enough for our cool kids to wear to their public schools).

In 2013, our February Preaching Rally had an important theme, so we donated a yellow t-shirt to each of the 400 attendees. Our teens reused these for camp that summer, but we also added a new shirt. The 2-color "Clean Up" shirts were a reminder of our new sermon series through 1 Corinthians, how that Paul was repeatedly telling the Corinthians to clean up their lives by fellowshipping with Jesus (1 Corinthians 1:8-9).

In 2014, we went all out... we had so many good ideas for t-shirts (and some extra financial donations), that we gave each teen TWO shirts. And, for the first time, we purchased **ladies fitted t-shirts** so that they did not have to end up swimming in their unisex tees again. The ladies shirts were extremely modest and looked feminine (equally important, in my opinion). Our ladies loved them, and we continue to spend the extra money to get the ladies shirts. The designs were a simple palm tree design on one (grey/orange), and a humorous "Respect the Hairlines of your youth staff" (complete with our receding hairlined silhouettes) on the other (red heather/white).

The next summer's t-shirts (2015) were themed "IDIOtS UNITE," a play on the Greek word (idios) for unique (as in idiosyncrasy) taken from 1 Corinthians 12:11. As unique, individual members, we are called to be a part of the local body—God's church (hence, *unite*).

Each shirt was intentionally designed and has its own unique story. Most of our teens wear their shirts proudly, portraying a Christian image and a good testimony of our church.

Tape Measure Questions

Lay out a 25' tape measure on the floor and pose questions to small groups of teens (ideally less than 20). Have them rate themselves by standing on the tape measure as a scale from 1-25. Notice how peer pressure influences them to change their minds or wait for the crowd. Ask probing questions that cause them to think of their answers. For example, if they are standing on #1 and say they are *extremely against* homosexuality, ask them, "Why?" Do not let them answer just because they think it is what the church believes. If they are going to be *extremely for* or *extremely against* something, they ought to have good reasons for it! Use it as a teaching time to instill leadership, choosing friends wisely, understanding peer pressure, standing on what you believe in, courage and more. Some sample ideas might be things like, "On a scale of 1-25, with 1 being extremely *against* it and 25 being extremely *for* it, how would you rate _____ (homosexuality, love of the Bible, divorce, etc. Or, start with silly things like Coke/Pepsi, bald youth pastors, etc.)

Calendars

Calendars help with all kinds of things, so we created a couple different calendars as Christmas presents for our teens.

Monthly calendar. I found a downloadable template for a simple half-sheet folded booklet calendar into which I could plug in our own pictures. Each month included a separate emphasis that coincides with the events of the month (e.g. Preaching Rally in February, Summer camp in July, etc.) with pictures and a couple sentences to think about.

Then, the daily squares were left blank. Teens were encouraged to get a marker and do the "Seinfeld" habit trick—each day you do something, mark a giant "X" across that day on your calendar. If you miss or skip a day, do not put an "X", and then see how many "X" days you can string in a row. Apparently, our brain hates to "break the chain," and seeing it on paper helps build the habit.

We encouraged the teens to mark an "X" for each day they read their Bibles and see how many days they can go without missing.

Honestly, I had no way to measure how much it was used, but it was easy to make and was one more tool that someone *might* use.

Daily tear-off calendar. In addition to the monthly calendar, we gave each teen a 365-day tear-off calendar that we printed and glued in-house. Everyone loves pictures, so I scoured our years of pictures and put in a different picture for each day. The season of the year corresponds to the events shown in the picture (e.g. pictures of past summer camps all through June and July). In addition, the youth activities and church events are printed in the notes section of the corresponding day.

I used each day's paper to mail a quick note to the teens or parents pictured, tracking the recipients on a spreadsheet. It was a simple discipline to force myself to write notes, and it was a nice encouragement to people when they received a picture of themselves or their kid and a thoughtful, intentional note from the youth pastor. I tried to make each note long and deliberate, yet warm and fun. I sometimes rattled off an inside joke and wrote only a couple words, but most of the time I was trying to communicate a lot of quality content, so I wrote small and carefully.

I found that it was a huge blessing to *me*. God used the daily calendars in our youth group, and I will repeat the idea in the future.

Wednesday "Big Day"

One year, we introduced a whole new Wednesday night format. We built up Halloween night to reveal three big surprises:

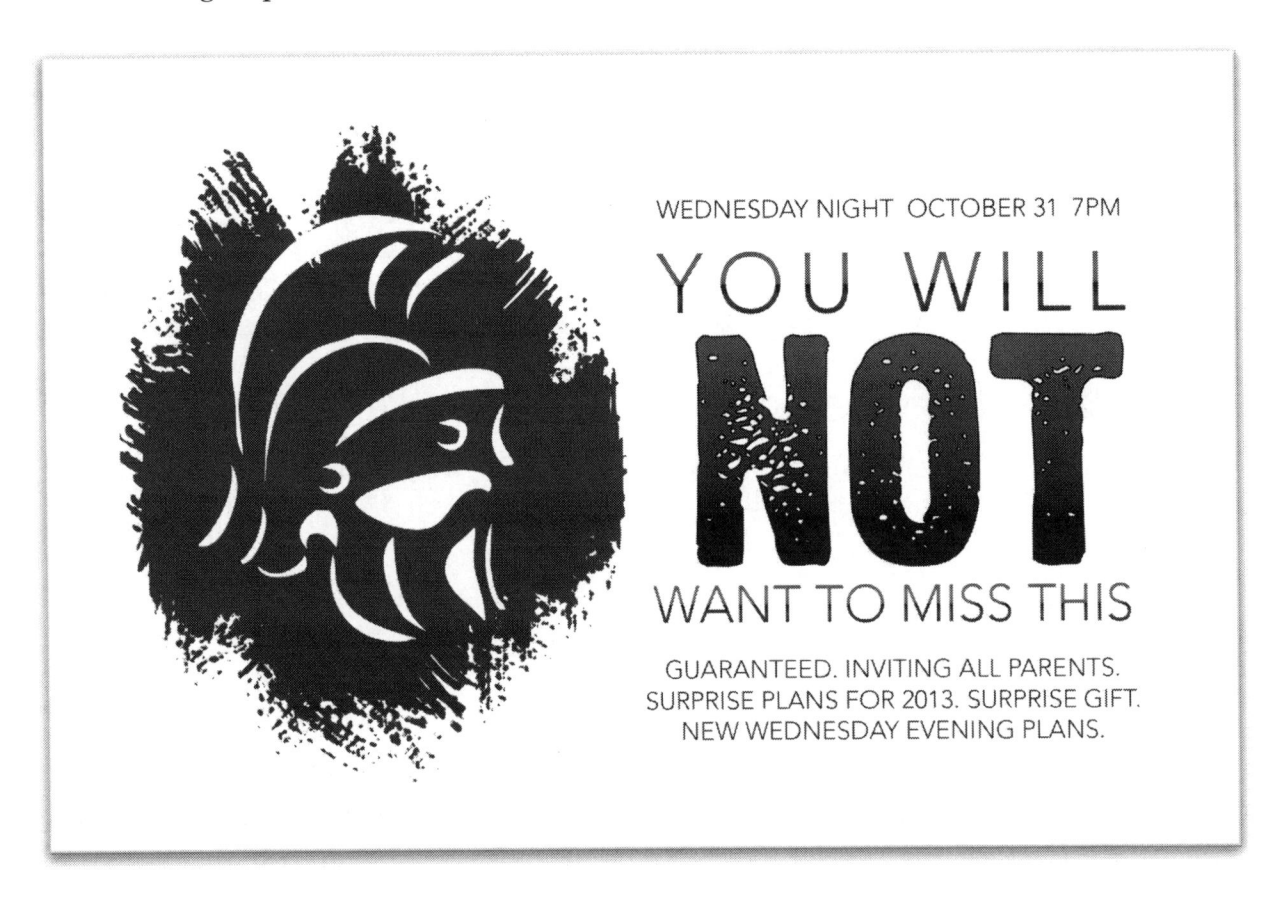

> **WEDNESDAY NIGHT OCTOBER 31 7PM**
>
> **YOU WILL NOT WANT TO MISS THIS**
>
> GUARANTEED. INVITING ALL PARENTS.
> SURPRISE PLANS FOR 2013. SURPRISE GIFT.
> NEW WEDNESDAY EVENING PLANS.

SURPRISE PLANS: Missions trip to Alaska for those who qualify.

SURPRISE GIFT: Free TOF devotional book *(see CalvaryBaptist.pub for details)*

NEW WEDNESDAY FORMAT: Described upcoming new format for Wednesdays (split class discussions over daily BIBS.)

MISSIONS TRIP

On our big night, I explained that we would take our first ever missions trip would go to a poor village in Alaska and conduct a Vacation Bible School.

Qualifying for the missions trip required daily, weekly and monthly requirem weekly church attendance on Wednesdays, and monthly soul-winning outrea

Teens filled out weekly requirement sheets and had to maintain an 1100-point average in order to qualify for the trip.

We waited several months before revealing the requirements for the trip in order to allow the teens time to get into the habit of daily BIBS devotions. Once we saw them being faithful on their own, we instituted the requirement sheets and points system for the Alaska trip. In essence, they began earning points for what they had been doing for months already: daily devotions and weekly church attendance.

The reasoning behind this came partly from the book *Drive* by Daniel Pink. The missions trip was meant more to be a "Now that..." type of reward instead of an "If... then..." type. Several reasons for this process are detailed in the book, but the main reason that I emphasized all throughout the process was that we DON'T do our devotions in order to go on the Alaska trip. *Points* are not the reason to have a relationship with God—the relationship is the reason.

SUMMARY

Each area announced at our "Big Day" overlapped the others. The daily BIBS became a requirement for the Alaska Missions Trip, and the Wednesday night classes became the weekly checkup for the requirements.

Whether the teens realized it or not, the daily BIBS format helped them immensely. They had mature discussions and proved themselves faithful over the series.

The whole program was a beneficial process not only for the group but for the individuals. I believe that if teens will grasp the concepts of Bible study now, they will be set for life.

Homiletics

For a 6-month time, three guys came to my office every week for a homiletics class. There was a senior, a junior and an 8th grader, and they took weekly quizzes, turned in weekly assignments and were involved in the weekly discussions.

Two of them were already called to preach, and the third is allowing the Lord to mold him. All three of them had a heart to learn and grow, and responded well to learning how to preach.

Rather than throw them into the experience of preaching without knowing *how*, I wanted to train them a little deeper than a short little 15-minute preacher-boy pep talk training time. I wanted to say more than "preach what the Lord lays on your heart." I wanted these young men to know how to properly handle God's Word. I wanted them to have the confidence that they were truly communicating a message from God and not rehashing something they'd heard before.

To accomplish this, we went page by page through Haddon Robinson's *Biblical Preaching* book, the book I learned to preach from. It is simple to understand and profoundly deep, at times. What I appreciated most was that we were not learning a sermon *structure*. After 10 weeks into the class, they never learned a thing about outlining. All discussions up to that point were answering the question, "What is God saying?" We spent the most time on finding the CIT (Central Idea of the Text) and clearly stating it both in the biblical world *and* the present world.

The meetings were one of the highlights of my week. It took a lot of preparation in reading, preparing quizzes, grading papers, etc., but it was a blast! I love preaching, and I love talking about preaching, so this class is a weekly rehash of all I love.

I am hoping that love spills over to the guys, too.

I will repeat the class whenever I have another few young men who would be interested and available to do it.

7. Books

My favorite gift/benefit since 2016 has been a monthly allowance for books. At our staff planning retreat, I mentioned to my dad (and pastor) that what I would REALLY like is more training. I want my preaching, my leading, my writing, and my overall effectiveness in ministry to improve, and I cannot do it alone. I knew books could help. Without hesitation, he granted me a simple allowance that I have used ever since.

I read physical and eBooks occasionally, but primarily listen to audiobooks from Audible.com and Audiobooks.com because of the ease of consuming content. Every time I am driving alone or doing yard work, I am listening to an audiobook.

This chapter is a review of new and old books that I have worked through. Each section is sorted roughly **in the order I enjoyed them** (favorite books listed first).

Please understand that these book reviews do NOT represent my endorsement of the author or content of each book.

Christian/Ministry

In 2014, God convicted me about my reading habits. For whatever reason, I had not read a Christian book in a long time (besides commentaries). I distinctly remember completing a certain book and searching for a new one when the thought struck me. *Hey... why am I not reading more Christian material?* That's when I purchased and read *The Pursuit of God*.

I now try to always be in a book that will deepen my walk with God. I plan on rereading old college books or leaning on recommended reading lists. One such list is included in each edition of the *Global Baptist Times* magazine, a bimonthly publication produced by my former pastor, Pastor Wayne Hardy. Each magazine includes three book reviews on various topics as well as a page full of "Stimulating Snippets," or quotes from several different books.

The following are some of my favorite Christian books from the past few years:

Knowing God

By J. I. Packer. This is my new favorite theology book. Packer exposes personal faults by drawing the reader closer to God through common doctrines. Although it is a deeply doctrinal book (it works its way through several of the core doctrines of the Bible), it can be approached devotionally. Meaning, rather than being a dry systematic theology (i.e. Bancroft), it is a thought provoking and awe-inspiring read. I highly recommend this book.

The Courage to Be Protestant

By David Wells. While *Knowing God* is my new favorite personal theology book, *The Courage to Be Protestant* is my new favorite Ecclesiology book. If you care about truth and are concerned with the direction that modern churches are taking it, read this book. It is a bleak and somewhat hopeless task—humanly speaking—to contend for truth, but this book provides solid arguments that show that truth will erode if we are not careful. *Courage...* is a compilation of four of Mr. Wells' previous books.

The Pursuit of God

By A. W. Tozer. This was one of those books I should have read a long time ago and never got around to. Finally, one day I read it and loved it. It is a delightful and insightful theological book packed with introspective questions. It probes deeper than any book I have read in a long time, and I needed its insight.

I Am a Church Member

By Thom Rainer. This practical and simple book has been the foundation of a simple series I preached to our church. In a day when church membership is downplayed, this book goes through several aspects of what church membership should look like. It is basic and, at times, weak on Scripture (using sparse one-verse proof-texts on some points), but I used the creeds and the structure of the book as the basis of my sermon series.

Love and Respect

By Dr. Emerson Eggerichs. Finally, a marriage book that puts the poor *man's* thoughts into words! This is not a beat-the-husband-up-for-not-communicating book. It is a balanced, biblically-based and well-researched book on 2-way communication in marriage. It has been a trending marriage book for several years, and the series keeps expanding to other relationships (see the book called *Mothers and Sons*, for example.) I highly recommend *Love and Respect* for your next marriage book.

Biblical Youth Work

Biblical Youth Work by Jim Krohn is a clear, biblical approach to various topics pertaining to youth groups including staff, parents, series and more. You will never have to guess the author's stance on each topic. I appreciate his firm convictions and well-worded philosophies, and pass on this recommendation of my college textbook.

Purposeful Parenting

By Pastor Troy Dorrell. Pastor Dorrell has conducted family and parenting seminars all over America using his material called *Purposeful Parenting*. His 50-page workbook coincides with four MP3 lessons on raising children. I have been through the series twice, and each time has been a help to me as a father of 2 kids. The seminar is available by contacting Eastland Baptist Church, Tulsa, OK, or by visiting bookstore. heartlandbaptist.edu.

Forward in The Face of Fear

Autobiography of missionary Edgar Feghaly.

Abdel felt the shudder of the not so distant battle as he prayed for the gas to pump faster. It barely trickled out, like a garden hose turned halfway on. When fighting intensified in Lebanon in the 1980's, the locals hoarded gasoline, never knowing how long the next battle would last.

Come on, come on, Abdel thought as the fuel dribbled into his dust-covered four seater car's gas tank.

Behind him, a man honked his horn. Anxious. No, scared.

Abdel (*fictional name—Edgar Feghaly's assistant pastor*) fumbled with his wallet, paid the cashier and jumped in the car, glancing in the mirror as he sped away. The nervous man was fueling his car now.

Abdel rounded the corner one block away, glancing back at the station as a building blocked his view.

He heard the explosion of a mortar. It sounded like it was right behind him. The smoke plumed from the gas station where he had fueled his car only moments before.

The man in the car behind him had been nervous for good reason. The mortar struck the very pump that Abdel had used.

This was life in Lebanon.

Three decades earlier, missionaries taught Edgar the meaning of the Gospel, showing that the Catholic faith was hopeless and helpless, and that Christ was sufficient to save people from their sins. As a boy, Edgar heard the truths—week after week—but listened to his fears and did not respond to the conviction.

One day as he played in his yard, without warning, Edgar was thrown into a cartwheel spin by a bomb explosion and landed in a heap. Dirt flew everywhere. Dust filled the air. His mom and all the neighbors flooded the street where Edgar was lying stunned. Everyone all at once was asking, "Are you okay, Edgar?" and saying things like, "Where did that bomb come from?"

The raucous made Edgar realize that he could have been killed by the rogue bomb. Although Beirut was relatively safe in those days, civil war was brooding and random bombings like this were not uncommon.

That night, under the Holy Spirit's conviction that *now* was the time of salvation, he awoke at midnight and called on the Lord to save him. His life changed forever.

Forward in the Face of Fear details the spiritual journey of Lebanese church planter Edgar Feghaly and the various difficulties he faced in his war-ravaged home town. As a compilation of stories grouped around certain topics in each chapter, the book is a chronology of Dr. Feghaly's journey through salvation, surrender, Bible college, pastoring, and helping others. His latter years of life have been spent helping international ministries.

Dr. Feghaly writes in a clear tone, never praising himself or his own sacrifices. While autobiographies might seem to imply that the authors are impressed with themselves, THIS autobiography has not a hint of pride or self-promotion. Dr. Feghaly's devotion to the Lord, his love and care for his family, his sacrificial leadership of his church, his unbending stance on truth and his insatiable thirst for helping others know God is evident in this story of a miracle.

I sometimes think of missionaries as heroes. This book validates that belief.

But you know what Dr. Feghaly would say? "I'm no hero. I'm doing my reasonable service."

Along the journey of his life, Dr. Feghaly has never wavered. Boy, am I encouraged to be more like him and others who are like him already. You will be encouraged when you read it, too.

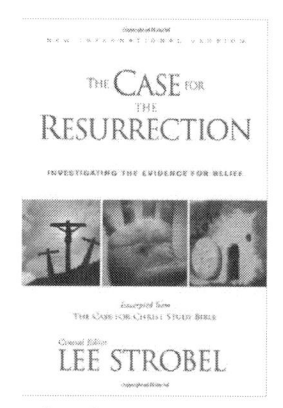

The Case for The Resurrection

By Lee Strobel. A few years ago, I read this whole book in one sitting in preparation for an Easter sermon. Strobel investigates the resurrection with the cunning of a journalist rather than the thoroughness of a researcher. Though thoroughly documented, it is not dry or overly academic. Strobel combines research and logic, laying out the evidence and building an airtight case for why the resurrection MUST be a literal, historical fact. The reader is left to decide for himself what he is to do with all the evidence piled in favor of the bodily death and resurrection of the historical man, Jesus. It is a wonderful and simple book I recommend as a quick overview of some key points of the Easter story.

Off Script

By Cary Schmidt. I read this book as soon as it was published (several years ago), and determined then that it would be the book I used for encouraging people in the middle of their battles with cancer. Bro. Schmidt wrote it *before* he knew his cancer was gone. The book is unique in that it is written amidst doctor visits, chemotherapy and big fat question marks like, "Am I going to live or die?" It is encouraging in its tone and message of hope, joy, and complete peace in God and His plan.

Pilgrim's Progress

By John Bunyan. This book is devotional and instructive. It is interesting to note the various struggles and tests we go through as Christians, and the allegorical format has been a nice change of pace from my personal reading habits (typically I only read non-fiction type books). This book is my in-between reading, but can be laborious, at times. I have to be in the right mood to read this book, as the unabridged version takes a while to get into.

Book Loaning Night

The following announcement sheet was from our Wednesday night class on September 18, 2013. I brought in a giant pile of books and let the teens borrow whichever ones they wanted. I took a picture (time and location stamped as it was taken from my iPhone) of each person with the book they borrowed in order to track who had what book.

RECOMMENDED READING

With these new little booklets coming out, *reading* has been on my mind lately. Are you a reader? You should be. It's much better for your brains than video games. When I was in high school, I read a bunch of fiction. In college, I moved to non-fiction. Now, most of my reading is non-fiction, and my shelves are full of helpful books. **If you ever want to borrow any, please let me know.** I'm serious. I hope you become readers. I brought a few samples tonight. Many of my books are written by people who do not believe exactly like us, but they have good points that we can learn from…

Biblical Preaching by Haddon Robinson. It's good if you're into preaching and Bible Study. It shaped my thinking on preaching God's Word, and is a required read at Heartland for the men.

Living by the Book by Howard Hendricks. It's a book on Bible study written for everyone, not just pastors. It is easy to understand and breaks down Bible study simply.

My Journey to Biblical Preaching is the story of Bro. Sam Davison's change from being a hard-nosed preacher to a Bible preacher. He tells the story of learning how to preach God's Word and how he desires to teach the young men of Heartland to preach.

America in Crimson Red by James Beller. It's a book on Baptist History in America and details the sacrifices of Baptists to shape what America is today.

The Calvary Road by Roy Hession is a short book that dives deep into spiritual self-examination.

Spiritual Leadership by J. Oswald Sanders has been a "textbook" for leaders for a long time. It is deep and will make you think introspectively. You'll read it and feel very... small. ☺ That's good.

Spiritual Leadership... The Interactive Study by Henry and Richard Blackaby is a question/answer type format book on leadership. It examines a lot of Bible and asks compelling questions for the reader to answer.

The 7 Habits of Highly Effective People by Stephen Covey is the book that everybody who's anybody reads. It's a classic. There is a teen version that is good, but this version takes you a little deeper.

How to Read Better and Faster by Norman Lewis is a book on speed-reading. It has charts that help you not only read faster but also comprehend what you're reading so you understand it! It helped me improve my read times within a few *minutes* of doing the drills.

Just Friends by Cary Schmidt and Mike Ray is a detailed book on relationships. It is an expanded version of my *A Case for Dating God's Way* booklet, and it will give you lots of Bible principles on dating.

Seven Royal Laws of Courtship by Pastor Jerry Ross is a booklet that gives several Bible principles on dating.

Stay in the Castle by Pastor Jerry Ross is a story for teen ladies who are waiting for God's timing in marriage. Mrs. Jamie read this in one of the split classes.

The Teenage Years of Jesus Christ by Pastor Jerry Ross is a Bible study and series of principles from Jesus' time on earth as a teenager.

The Far Side by Gary Larson. You can borrow my comic books if you're into them. ☺

Drawing Cartoons. If you're into doodling.

Sherlock Jones and the Missing Diamond by Ed Dunlop is a fiction mystery book written for older kids/younger teens. Even though they were written younger, I read all my Ed Dunlop books a couple times each all through high school. They're entertaining.

Readers are leaders. Leaders are readers. Cool people are readers. Bro. Garrett can't read [*context: one of our 2013 summer interns was Bro. Garrett Gayoso*]. Bro. Garrett's not cool. (Poor guy. He's not even here to defend himself!)

-Bro. Ryan

Preaching Books

A Man of God

I try to preach complete expository sermons each Sunday as if I were pastoring a church. As I give myself to the Word and faithfully feed "my" little flock (as I view my teens), I am helped and challenged, personally. I am convinced that the Word preached is God's avenue to communicate His truth to each generation, and I want my skill in the pulpit to constantly develop (and not only through experience!).

In the Old Testament, Elijah was a man of God. He preached God's truth to his generation in a confrontational manner. Not that his *spirit* was confrontational (some people view all preaching as anger, judging, or arrogance), but his *message* was contrary to the people's lifestyle, and therefore confrontational. When the people were confronted with their sin, they either turned to or away from God.

In the New Testament, John the Baptist preached the same way. He, too, was a man of God, and preached God's Word in a clear, confrontational way. When he came to prominence because of his preaching, people asked, *"What then? Art thou Elias? And he saith, I am not. Art thou that prophet? And he answered, No."* (John 1:21) It was as if people were shocked to hear his message, and it reminded them of the Old Testament prophets—thundering out God's Word to His people.

The culture of Elijah's day was different than the culture of John the Baptist's, but the Word never changed. It is no coincidence that the method of preaching did not change, either. The man of God took the Word of God and preached it to God's people, confronting them with God's truth, leaving them to decide what to do with the truth they had just received.

Today, we stand in similar roles—called to be men of God as youth directors, associate pastors, senior pastors, and Christian workers. We who are called to preach have the same obligation as John the Baptist, albeit to a whole new culture. While times and cultures might change, God's method of preaching has not.

One of the core principles of the youth ministry at our church is that we are intentional about developing young people who are passionate about God's Word. One way we try to accomplish this is to hold the ministry of preaching in high regard—keeping the pulpit hot.

Is every Sunday school sermon confrontational? Of course not. At least, not in the way you might think when you hear the term *confrontational*.

Every sermon is biblical, though. Every sermon, to the best of our ability, is clear. Every sermon takes the timeless truth from thousands of years ago, spans the ages, bridges the culture and time gap and applies it to teens living in 2015. Every sermon clearly articulates God's thoughts from the Word first, then takes those thoughts and makes them mean something to a homeschooled 7th grader and a graduate going to SDSU this Fall.

My main responsibility as a youth director is to lead the hearts of our church's teens to draw closer to God. My mission is accomplished when my teens are in love with God's Word—through preaching and their personal study. While I cannot control their personal devotional life, I can try to provide a youth environment where they are at least hearing God's voice a couple times a week through preaching.

Because of this weighty responsibility to be accurate and clear, I want to constantly grow in my preaching ministry. So, periodically I will read new books and revisit old ones.

The following is a short list of some of the books that have helped my preaching. Again, I do NOT endorse everything in these books (particularly since I exclusively use the KJV), and will only highlight my favorite aspects of each:

Biblical Preaching

By Haddon Robinson. This is the original book I studied when learning to preach. It follows the format of arriving at a "Big Idea" from each biblical text, then applying that to the hearers through preaching. It is strong on biblical content, but weak on arranging the ideas into a certain structure. Reading this book changed my life and shaped my passion for preaching, and I have gone through it with a few of my young men who are called to preach.

Invitation to Biblical Preaching

By Don Sunukjian. Every modern day sermon must follow the original author's thoughts in order to be accurate. Sunukjian does a masterful job of getting into the flow of the original author's thoughts and designing the entire structure of the sermon along this route. He provides several case study examples that build throughout the book, and his method is accurate and explained well. It can get technical, at times, but is a helpful read.

Living by the Book

By Howard Hendricks. This book is a masterful—albeit basic (in a good way!)—approach to hermeneutics. It is written to the student as a beginning manual, although the techniques are as deep as you can get in Bible study. Each chapter gives in-depth examples and Bible study tools, tips, and tricks relating to the chapter's topic. While *BIBS* is a good starting point for basic Bible study, *Living by the Book* is the next step in starter Bible study details.

Preaching with Freshness

By Bruce Mawhinney. This book provides exactly what the title promises—a freshness to the vital aspect of your youth ministry. The book is written in a story format, is easy to read, is inspiring and surprisingly instructional. It is a quick (two hour) read, yet incredibly helpful.

The Art and Craft of Biblical Preaching

Compiled by Haddon Robinson and Craig Larson. This collection of articles provides quick insights by dozens of authors. Each article is categorized and indexed by topic, providing a quick reference for topics such as hermeneutics, application, delivery, structure and more.

Why Johnny Can't Preach

By T. David Gordon. Dr. Gordon was diagnosed with cancer and was not expected to live. He wrote this book with a "What do I have to lose?" mentality. He bore his heart (and frustrations) to all who would read. In time, he was cured of the cancer, but the book was still published. It challenges some common errors in preaching (like ignoring the author's intent) and is a helpful little book, packed with conversational topics. This book is a great read, with no down-sides.

Bible Study (Software)

When I approach a new sermon series (usually through a book of the Bible), I browse for the best commentaries to help me study. Some of my processes and purchases have included the following:

BestCommentaries.com

My first step in finding commentary reviews is to look up BestCommentaries.com and search for the book of the Bible I am interested in. This website rates each major commentary and applies various tags and scores including Devotional, Technical, Pastoral, and Special Studies. Each book includes Amazon reviews as well as other thorough reviews, and shows the various websites and software programs that sell the book (i.e. Amazon.com, Olive Tree App, Logos software, etc.)

Olive Tree Bible App

With free apps for Mac, Windows, iOS and Android, the Olive Tree App is my go-to resource for all Bible study. I have spent WAY too much money on commentaries because, well, it is so easy! I sign into my Olive Tree account on any device, browse for the book I want, and click download.

With this app I can view Strong's references by tapping the word in the Bible, and I can view side-by-side comparison of the Scripture with the commentary that accompanies it. As I scroll in Scripture, the commentary scrolls too. In addition, all notes and highlights sync with all connected apps, so any work I do on my iPhone can update on my Mac, and vice versa.

KJV with Strong's References

This is the tab that is always open on the left panel. It includes one-touch popup definitions of each word. It was an inexpensive download through the Olive Tree Bible Study App.

Calvary Baptist Publications

Calvary Baptist Publications is a compilation of ministry resources originating from everyday church needs. Each book, booklet and minibook originated as a way to help our church–Calvary Baptist Church of Temecula, CA–and has since expanded to those beyond our local ministry.

The Preaching Rally

This book is "One youth pastor's take on how to plan and run a one-day youth conference." I wrote extensively on all the major categories of our Preaching Rally including theme, food, parking, schedule, music, gifts, registration, improvements and more. This book is the compilation of notes from hosting six Preaching Rallies over the years, and it will help you think through details for your own rally. *270 pages. $14.99 on Amazon.com*

From the back cover:

> *Every year, our church hosts a few hundred young people for the Preaching Rally. This book is how we do it.*
>
> *IF YOU HAVE FOUND yourself in charge of a big event, you have a lot of work to do. You have to first THINK about what to do, and then you have to DO it.* **Let this book help you.**
>
> *The PREACHING RALLY lays out the nuts and bolts of* **how we plan and run our one-day youth conference**, *and gives reasons behind each step. You will find detailed spreadsheets, our exact timeline of mailings, church meetings and more.*
>
> *Most of the frustrations of poorly-run events can be fixed with planning—thinking about the details and doing them. The PREACHING RALLY is* **years' worth of experience on paper**.
>
> *I hope it helps to you.*

BIBS: Big Idea Bible Study

What started as a sermon series on Bible study turned into a small spiral-bound BIBS devotionals that our youth group worked through. Later, I was approached about teaching a Bible class at a local Christian high school, so I worked my lesson notes into a book format and published the book to use as our class textbook. *BIBS* uses Howard Hendricks' "Observation, Interpretation, Application" method to interpret Scripture and arrive at a Big Idea, applying it to our everyday lives. It is written to help young people and seasoned Christians alike. See BIBSBibleStudy.com or "Chapter 1 – Sermon Series" for more information. *226 pages. $13.99 on Amazon.com*

From the back cover:

Have you ever been reading a book and had your eyes glaze over? All of a sudden you realize you have been staring at the same paragraph for 10 minutes but have not read a word. Or, you might have read it, but you sure did not get it!

We have all been there. Some people do that with every book. Every time they sit to read, their mind wanders away.

On top of that, your pastor gets up on Sunday and says, "You should spend time in God's Word. Read your Bible this week."

"Yeah right," you think. "I can barely understand the Bible. It does not make sense to me. I don't get it."

It does not have to be that way. You CAN read the Bible AND understand what it says. It is not impossible; it just takes a format that works for you.

That is what this book is all about. BIBS (Big Idea Bible Study) is a format designed for every Christian. It is a Bible study method that takes you into the depths of Scripture but also keeps sight of the bigger picture.

*BIBS is a **simple step-by-step course** to help you discover what God is saying in His Word. You will learn to observe, interpret and apply Scriptural truth, taking the "old, dry, boring" book and discovering the life it promises for your soul.*

BIBS Devotional: One-Year

The *BIBS Devotional Book* is a daily Bible reading and study plan. It is designed to guide the reader in both an in-depth study of a certain short passage every day, as well as weekly overview readings of the surrounding chapters to provide context. The *BIBS Devotional: One-Year* edition covers the following books: 1 Thessalonians, Romans, Daniel, Philippians, James, Ruth and 1 Corinthians. Because of the variety of genres and topics, this is a great book for anyone who likes variety AND biblically deep truths. Further, because this book is divided neatly into 2-week cycles, the reader can choose the sections which suit his or her needs best. *274 pages. $11.99 on Amazon.com*

From the inside pages of the *BIBS Devotionals:*

The BIBS Daily Devotional is a daily Bible reading and study plan. It is designed to guide the reader in both an in-depth study of a certain short passage every day, as well as weekly overview readings of the surrounding chapters to provide context.

Note from the author: "There are two main reasons I do not often use or recommend most devotional books or most things written for teens. First, they cater to this false idea that teens are somehow less intelligent and need things 'dumbed down' for them to get it. Wrong! Those in their teen years are highly motivated to excel at whatever they are challenged to do. BIBS simply challenges them to know their Bibles if they are up to it.

"Second, most devotionals have the reader read little of the Bible and think little for himself. Then, if there is a biblical text to read–and sometimes it is only one verse(!)–the devotional tells the reader what to think about that text. God's Word IS saying something

in every text, but discovering it for myself and applying it to myself produces more lasting results. Following the BIBS format offers both the depths of Scripture AND the flow of thought of the context of Scripture. It is a guide to help you hear from God and a tool to help you understand and apply His desires for your life."

BIBS Devotional: Proverbs

This devotional is a 30-week study through highlights from each chapter of Proverbs. Proverbs is succinct, simple and practical. While the average reader might typically follow the Proverb-a-day method of Bible reading, the red *BIBS Daily Devotional* will take him deeper into the truths he so often breezed over. At times, the reading covers whole chapters, while other days only cover one or two verses. This is a great starter book for those looking into the BIBS method of Bible study. *150 pages. $8.99 on Amazon.com*

Interning Well

Since 2013, our church has hosted two college students as our church interns. We meet almost daily to hand out tasks and follow up on projects. These meetings produce rich training times, which we follow up with written articles on the topic. After three years, we combined these articles into topics and bound them in a book, available on Amazon.com. *190 pages. $12.99 on Amazon.com*

From the back cover:

> *INTERNS ARE MORE THAN GOPHERS ("go for" this and "go for" that). At least, they should be. Secular internships are about gaining business knowledge through hands-on experience. The same is true for church internships. Your goal as an intern should be to learn as much as possible through the experience of ministering to others—church staff and church members. Your internship is more than door-knocking and lawn-mowing. It is more than all the "stuff" that goes into ministry. Your internship is about learning. Take advantage of that.*
>
> *This book was birthed from our daily intern staff meetings. I was never a summer intern, but I was a staff intern for two years under Pastor Wayne Hardy (Bible Baptist Church, Stillwater, OK). I try to cram my two years into the 12 weeks with our interns. Poor guys. After each activity or event, we discuss the details and provide training. Sometimes the training is instruction, correction or rebuke. Sometimes it is embarrassing. Sometimes it is awkward. All of it, though, is intended to edify—to strengthen and build up—the intern. It is intended to create a ministry-minded, servant-hearted future church staff member. As an intern, learn as much as you can. Do all you can to be a blessing and help to others. Serve. Lead. Grow. Change. INTERN WELL.*

A Case for Being Timeless

The theme for one of our Preaching Rallies was *Timeless*, and we encouraged the teens to stick to the timeless truths of God's Word rather than chase every new fad that sweeps the culture. This book was donated to every attendee of that conference. *150 pages. $9.99 on Amazon.com*

From the back cover:

DO YOU WANT TO BE A LAB RAT?

I don't. Who would?

But that is exactly what the youth of today are: lab rats. Modern church leaders use the youth—not the elderly—as their lab rats. New church fads are tested on those who have not lived long.

New is not always bad... but it is always new. It is never time-tested. It is never "tried and true." We never know if "new" will work, because it does not have a history.

Before trusting the new fads that sweep through modern churches, I want to anchor my beliefs to something TIMELESS. I want to know that that the path I am on has proved to be right. I don't want to be a lab rat. Do your tests on someone else.

I choose to be TIMELESS.

Love God, Love Others, Do Right

The Teens of Faith have been my life and ministry since 2010. Since day one, in every class (Sundays and Wednesdays), the teens have received a note in their announcement sheets. This is a compilation of those notes. *279 pages. $14.99 on Amazon.com*

A Case for Bible College

This book is a 2-part look at why our church encourages our teens to attend a year of Bible college. It originated as a simple course to help prepare students for Bible college and grew into a full book. Part One is written to the parents and shows WHY we encourage Bible college. Part Two is written to help the prospective student know how to prepare – financially, academically, spiritually, etc. *188 pages. $12.99 on Amazon.com*

From the back cover:

> EVER CONSIDERED BIBLE COLLEGE? Whether you have or you have not, A Case for Bible College is for you. You might wonder, "What's the big deal about Bible College, anyway? What's the point?"

Or, you might already be planning to go but you want to know more about how to prepare. Either way, this book will help you.

PART ONE is all about building a case for why many churches encourage high school graduates to attend at least one year of Bible College. Part One details many of the benefits, considers a few objections and discusses several biblical principles on choosing a Bible College. Part One is written primarily to parents and those who are not yet convinced of the need for Bible College.

PART TWO is written to the prospective student and is meant to help prepare him or her for the distinct new culture of Bible College. Part Two helps the student navigate many of the changes that will take place in the first year of Bible College: spiritual, academic and social, to name a few.

The BONUS CHAPTER at the end is written specifically to those students who have chosen to attend Heartland Baptist Bible College in Oklahoma City. This chapter provides a quick look at a few Heartland-specific topics that will not apply to other Bible Colleges.

"A Case for..." Minibooks

Explanation: "A Case for..." is a series of booklets that were written to provide a practical approach to various topics addressed in our church. We print and finish our own little booklets at our church and distribute them for free in a display rack in our church foyer.

Origins: Each booklet originally started either as a sermon or as a sermon series, and some of the notes were written out and printed into a booklet form. They have been adapted for a broader audience including all adults, but the foundation of each booklet so far was directed at teens.

Effectiveness: It is nice to have already thought through a topic and to be able to simply hand someone a booklet instead of going into a long conversation with reasons. Further, people that are searching and digging for answers can often find them by reading, and we want to facilitate that as much as possible.

To simply know that the church leadership has taken the time to write out reasons for doing what they do, whether certain church members agree or not, they *at least* have to know that the church is not haphazard about their ministries nor are they doing "stuff" without knowing why.

Minibooks:

A Case for Saturday Soul-Winning. Every Saturday, our church goes into the community to spread the gospel through our door-to-door soul-winning program. While our main focus is on obeying the Great Commission, several other factors are at play each week, as well. *A Case for Saturday Soul-winning* is a minibook spelling out a few fun reasons to come to our organize Saturday soul-winning time. It does not go into all the biblical reasons and motivations; it simply provides a logical case to be considered.

A Case for Reverence. Most church services today are laid back. *A Case for Reverence* is a practical explanation of why we conduct our services in more of a formal environment. Often guests are pleased with the level of respect but sometimes might wonder *why* that type of spirit is there—why we sing hymns, spend time preaching, discourage distractions and are generally "different" than basically all other churches in our town.

A Case for Why We Have "Church" is a look at the foundation of why we do what we do... church. "Where did this whole 'church' thing come from, anyway? What about para-church organizations?

Aren't all churches the same?" This minibook explains the difference between *biblical legitimacy* and *effectiveness*. Lots of ministries are *effective* and help people, but a proper church is the only *biblically legitimate* ministry that has God's approval through His authority.

A Case for Dating God's Way. Hoping to save teens a lot of future heartache, this minibook was written to help navigate some of life's questions on biblical dating. Should I date? How do I start? Read the book to find out!

A Case for Sunday Evening Church. "Weeell... attendance is down so we'll just cancel our Sunday night services." Should you? This minibook gives a few solid reasons why our church still believes in the Sunday evening service.

Encourage Your Pastor

October is Pastor Appreciation month, but our church has rarely done many special things for our pastor. Since I am Pastor's son, I felt that it was out of line for me to head up any kind of special gift for him. Instead, I preached to the church on a topic that is sometimes neglected by our humble pastor—the church's role and the pastor's role.

I preached the morning and evening services on a Sunday in August, as well as the following Wednesday. My parents were out of town and I was filling the pulpit, so I used it as an opportunity to preach a topic that might be awkward if Pastor were present.

In addition, we compiled and printed hundreds of booklets to hand to each attendee. Each booklet contained several articles I had been collecting for months—articles about encouraging your pastor.

I have bundled these articles along with all three sermon notes into one PDF document (about 40 MB). If you would like these valuable articles, visit cbctemecula.org/share/encourage.zip *and it will download automatically to your computer. For direct access to the PDF, visit* cbctemecula.org/share/Encourage-Your-Pastor.pdf

PDF includes:

- *Full booklet of encouraging articles*
- *Sermon: 1 Thessalonians 5 – The church's duty to their pastor*
- *Sermon: Luke 17:10 – The pastor's duty as a servant*
- *Sermon: Various passages – The pastor's role in the church*

Booklets By Pastor W. M. Rench

Call Calvary Baptist Church directly to order any of the following booklets, (951) 676-8700:

Imminent! The Return of Jesus Christ

This booklet lays out the Scriptures and builds a case for why Christ's return could happen at any moment. It is available free to our church in our book rack. If you want a PDF copy, please contact me directly through my website at RyanRench.com.

Islam

Around the time that Muslims were seeking to build a mosque near Ground Zero, ground-breaking ceremonies were beginning on the 5-acre plot of land next door to our church for another Mosque. Pastor Rench was on CNN discussing the effects of Islam on America, and wrote this follow-up booklet to highlight some of Islam's teachings from their Quran.

Enduring Sound Doctrine

At times, error creeps into churches through outside influences. A pastor that cares for his sheep will warn against false doctrine, encouraging the flock to "endure sound doctrine," as Paul taught. This booklet details some of the errors of home churches, the Pearl family, and others who lift certain teachings above the importance of the church.

Skip the Sermon, Worship at Home?

In our area of Southern California, and with the prevalence on online and other media options for church, some Christians are convinced that home worship is the same as church worship. This booklet gives several warnings against home church gatherings that are replacing the assemblies of people in true churches.

Classic Christianity

Pastor Rench received an advertisement in the mail promoting another rock concert. He remembered his past with rock music with shame. To his surprise, the advertisement was for a church, although the appearance was worldly. This booklet contrasts classic, timeless Christianity against the modern, changing fads of today's contemporary Christianity.

Is Sunday School Biblical?

A hot topic among home-church advocates these days is, "Is Sunday School biblical?" The question is sincere. While Sunday School is certainly not *anti*-biblical (there is no clear teaching *against* it directly), to say that it is *un*-biblical (in that it is not even mentioned) is also incorrect. This booklet shows the biblical precedent of Sunday School.

Calvary Chapel: What's the Difference?

Our church is often mistaken with a church called Calvary Chapel, a non-denominational church with several locations and schools across Southern California. Because of the confusion between our church and theirs, Pastor Rench clarifies the differences in Bible doctrines and practices.

Gender

Why Gender Matters

By Leonard Sax. Dr. Sax is both a medical doctor and a psychiatrist. His take on gender is secular but well-researched. This book is written mostly to parents and teachers, but is applicable to ministry. Much of his research provides solid data outside the Bible. This can be helpful when dealing with the unsaved over the gender neutrality issues pervading our culture today. Recommended with the understanding that this is a secular book.

Girls On the Edge

By Leonard Sax. Written by the same author as *Why Gender Matters*, this book was a follow-up that delves deeper into girl-specific issues, symptoms and solutions. Dr. Sax uses graphic language to describe current struggles and trends in high school today. It is shocking yet eye-opening, and this book is recommended with reservations. Dr. Sax is certainly writing from a secular, humanistic mindset and tries to control problems with secular fixes.

Boys Adrift

By Leonard Sax. Dr. Sax's focus in this book is "the 5 factors driving the growing epidemic of unmotivated boys and underachieving young men." I see *exactly* these problems in our youth group, and his book validated my personal stance against aspects of video games, ADD, ADHD, and more. As a Medical Doctor, he offers lots of data and research through his practice. He gives a secular perspective to the Bible truth that preachers have been preaching for generations. I *loved* this book and read it in hours. Our guys responded to a passionate sermon based on this data and the message of 1 Corinthians 16:9-13 "Grow up." Highly recommended book.

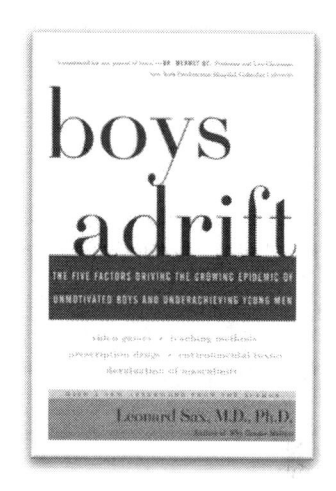

Leadership – Historical

After hearing from several different people (authors, preachers, business men, secular and Christian leaders) that I ought to vary my reading, I knew there must be something to it. Instead of my usual reading habits, I expanded to other genres.

I am glad I did. Ultra-glad.

I wholly recommend varying your reading. It broadens your knowledge base and exposes you to new worlds you never knew existed. We can get locked in on one particular genre or style of reading, and we miss the variety of life. At least… that is what I did! Now I strive to read several different types of books.

The following sections include secular books on from a variety of categories:

Up from Slavery

By Booker T. Washington. I get "new favorites" a lot, and this is one of my new favorites. Something about Mr. Washington's writing and leadership style resonates with me, and I admire him tremendously. I love his humility, sincerity, and resolve no matter the circumstances. Booker T. Washington was enslaved as a boy, taught himself to read in his spare time, worked hard as a young freed man, got further education and later went on to lead one of the nation's leading universities and becoming a national and international icon. This book is his incredible story.

Character Building

By Booker T. Washington. In leading the Tuskegee Institute, Booker T. Washington held a weekly assembly where he trained the students in character, discipline, and practical moral living. This book is a collection of the speeches that he gave to his students. While it was not a Christian university, his principles are Christian-based and thoroughly biblical. His patience with the students shows in how minutely he instructed them, from learning to make their beds or brush their teeth to sustaining themselves after college and creating a new family legacy.

R. E. Lee On Leadership

By H. W. Crocker. One of my top five mentors, Bro. Sam Davison, says that this is his favorite book on leadership. In his opinion, we can throw out every other leadership book and just read this one, it is so good. While I do not agree that we can throw *all* other books out, I do highly recommend it. It is more than biography as it intersperses leadership lessons, summarizing Lee's principled life and pulling out timeless nuggets that can still help us today. It is refreshing to read after men who lived in a different world, yet whose lives can still impact us centuries later.

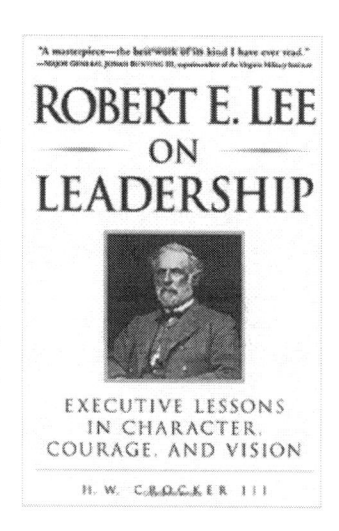

The Second World War: Milestones to Disaster

By Winston Churchill. I love books that open my mind to new worlds I never knew existed. Sometimes, history is more unbelievable than fantasy. Such is the case with Winston Churchill's viewpoint of the political events that took place between World War I and World War II. Hitler was, apparently, a brilliant manipulator and a long-term strategist. He exploited the unstable politics of his day, sidestepped international laws, and rebuilt Germany into a fighting force—all under the noses of the rest of the world! In this book, Winston Churchill documents his own warnings to England's parliament, and describes his decades-long battle with other British politicians. Churchill tried to warn the British people of the impending war, but it was too late before Great Britain responded. By the time the war broke out, Churchill was the natural leader for Great Britain, keeping all of Europe struggling along until finally the reluctant United States joined the war.

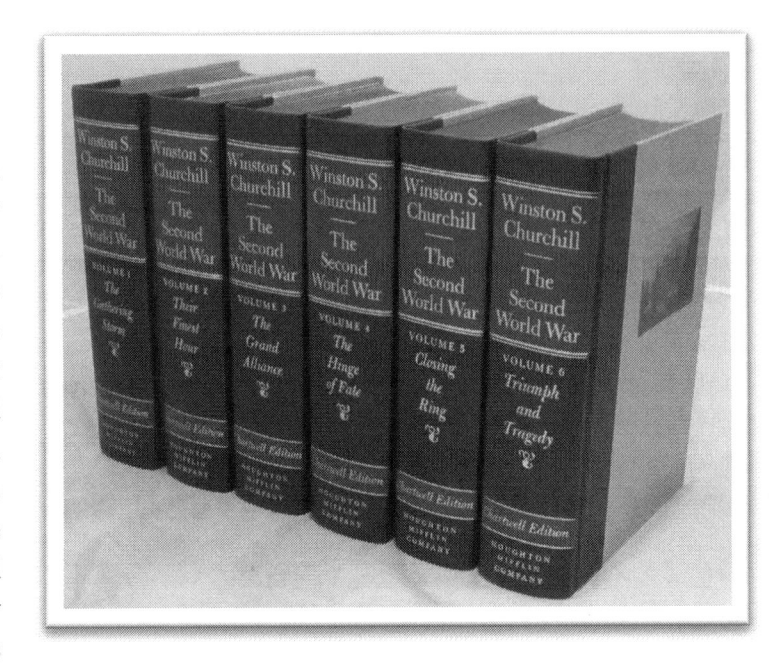

This book goes to the source, as Winston Churchill's own magnificent leadership and communication skills show us his key perspective on how the Great War came to be. It is an astounding read, although technical and somewhat overly detailed in spots. If you like information, this will intrigue you.

Originally, Churchill released his history in six volumes (pictured above) and later condensed them to four: *1. Milestones to Disaster, 2. Alone, 3. The Grand Alliance, 4. Triumph and Tragedy.*

Personal Memoirs of U. S. Grant

I had preconceptions about the Civil War based on what I learned in elementary school. While I appreciate my upbringing, I am not closed to new perspectives. No one thing in this book was life-changing, but it is intriguing to read from the mind of one of the leading generals of the Civil War—going straight to the source. This, and the other Civil War era books mentioned, helped me understand the history, motivations and circumstances of the Civil War much better. Though informative, the memoirs of U. S. Grant are sometimes dry, and are not meant to be a full autobiography or a detailed account of the war.

Leadership – Modern

Extreme Ownership

By Navy SEALs Jocko Willink and Leif Babin. Although profane at times, using the foul language typical of most Navy SEALs, the principles of this book resonated with me. In fact, it was probably my favorite book of 2015. First, I am always impressed by experts in any field, and SEALs are top performers in their world. Second, the idea of ownership has been one that I have always been passionate about. This book takes it—well—to the extreme (see what I did there?). Each chapter starts with a true story from a Navy SEAL's combat experience and relates that principle of leadership to everyday business affairs. In my opinion, profane SEALs are often more principled than many Christians when it comes to extreme ownership. I needed the kick in the pants.

EntreLeadership

By Dave Ramsey. This is one of my favorite business books of all. Dave Ramsey's intentionally Christian approach to life and business is a refreshing look at "success." His book details a lot of his company's hiring process, their daily processes, and their core values. It was a challenge to me, personally, to be more intentional about my life and ministry.

Tribes

By Seth Godin. This is a classic Seth Godin book—high on philosophy and intentionally low on practicality. I appreciate this style of writing and tend to think that way, so I enjoyed this book. It is motivational, spurring the reader to take action and do what he knows he should be doing. For us as Christians, this means doing what God has called us to do with all our might. This book easily translates to Christian ministry, but is far too self-centered to be recommended as a ministry manual.

Good Leaders Ask Great Questions

By John C. Maxwell. This was the first and only full John Maxwell book I have ever read, but I liked it so much, I immediately began reading it again. I became an immediate John Maxwell fan from this book because of his transparency, honesty, sincerity and experience. His writing is easy to read and packed with valuable statements. Although some of his quips might sound cliché, they are nonetheless profound, regardless of how often you have heard them stated elsewhere. In the past (before I had read a full book of his), I thought of Maxwell as shallow and self-centered, and I questioned how one man could write so much about one narrow topic. I see, now. His personal stories, tactics, and helpful arguments were beneficial, to say nothing yet about the content of the book. I came across a podcast interview of him, heard him reference this book, purchased it and read it within a week. I learned much about questions, and thoroughly enjoyed this book.

Historical Narrative

Unbroken

By Laura Hillenbrand. I am realizing I have a lot of favorites. This book is my favorite, too. If you are into "thrillers," this one will blow the others away, because it is a true story. *Unbroken* chronicles the story of Louis Zamporini, an Olympian on track to break the 4-minute mile before he was drafted in the war, stranded at sea under record circumstances, nearly killed in a POW camp and finally released from prison, sin and ultimate bitterness. *Unbroken* is by far **the most incredible, unbelievable true story** I have ever read.

1776

By David McCullough. My wife and I bought this book for my dad back when it first got popular, but we never read it ourselves. Even if you are not into history, this book is so compelling and so insightful, you are sure to enjoy it. You are drawn into the story of the revolution as the author takes you through the worst year of the war for America's independence— 1776. Although it was the year of our declaration of independence, it was a bleak time in America's history. This book gives renewed appreciation for our country's founders and struggle for independence.

Endurance: Shackleton's Incredible Voyage

By Alfred Lansing. For an incredible story on the same level as Laura Hillenbrand's *Unbroken* (my all-time most incredible story I have ever read), read *Endurance*. Shackleton's leadership of his bedraggled crew after being stranded on the ice of Antarctica is incredible. Suffering frostbite and starvation along every step of the journey, the story of what happened to the crew will leave you wondering if the story is true (yet it is!). For a story to challenge your own resilience, grit, stamina, and bodily endurance, read *Endurance: Shackleton's Incredible Voyage*.

The Wright Brothers

By David McCullough. I read another of McCullough's books, *1776*, and enjoyed it so much, I wanted to read more of his work. McCullough thoroughly researches his subjects, pouring over personal diaries, letters, local newspapers of the era, and every book written about the subject. His research is a mountain of clay, but his book is a perfectly carved sculpture—a work of art with every detail perfectly in place. Not too much; not too little. He carves away just enough for the work to not be overwhelming, yet what he leaves is meaty in detail.

The Wright Brothers is a creative nonfiction book, meaning it is a historical account written like a novel. Rather than conveying dry facts, the writing style tells a story. *The Wright Brothers* gives not only the character and history of the two brothers and their work, but goes on to explain what they did with the rest of their lives. The book was enjoyable to read, but because it was about a subject that was less important to me than, say, the American Revolution, I found it less impacting than *1776*.

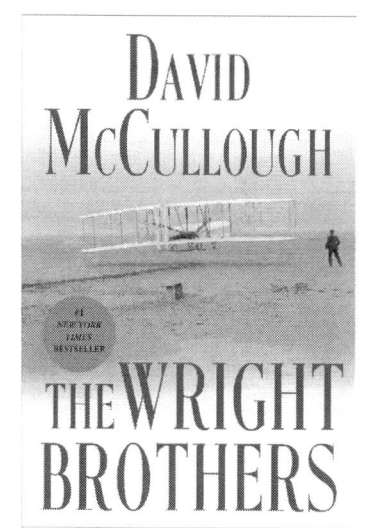

Writing

*Having worked on my writing more than almost anything else, I feel like I am only getting worse at it; not better. *sigh. These books have helped me... some. Hopefully.*

The Elements of Style

By William Strunk and E. B. White. Do not judge this book by its cover. As style manuals go, this one is a standard. While not everyone agrees with all the rules and exceptions of the English language, we can all appreciate this English professor's passion for words. After reading this book, I realized how horrible a writer I am (!). I personally loved the book and recommend to anyone who is interested in writing.

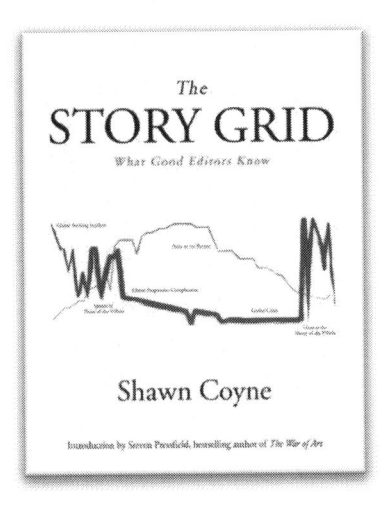

Story Grid

By Shawn Coyne. After decades as an editor in all the big publishing houses, Coyne needed a framework for his high-profile clients to understand what to change in their story, and why. He created *The Story Grid* as a language that author and editor can use in multiple genres to know what works (and what does not) in a story. I have read most, but not all, of this book, and have combined my reading with podcast listening on this topic. I appreciate men who are so ridiculously far ahead of me that it would take the same decades of experience to match their wit. When they are willing to share their experience, I am willing to listen. That is what *The Story Grid* is all about—decades of editorial experience compiled in a structured format.

APE: Author Publisher Entrepreneur

By Guy Kawasaki. If you are interested in self-publishing a book, *APE* is the all-inclusive guide. It is the most up-to-date and one of the only exhaustive resources on the subject. He details all the major websites that offer self-publishing and provides step by step instructions on setting up and producing your book from start to finish. Instructions include eBooks and print books. This book is strongly recommended for anyone considering self-publishing.

Your First 1000 Copies

By Tim Grahl. As the title suggests, this book is a guide to self-publishing and marketing a book. I liked the narrow focus of the content because, while it was written for beginners, it did not try to give the WHOLE process from start to finish. In addition, I like the repetition of the most important points like serving your audience and building an email list. Further, I like that Grahl gives relevant examples and recommendations on his website for things like graphic designers, email clients, and more. This is a good starting point from an author I am familiar with after listening to his "Story Grid Podcast" and reading his blog.

Personal Growth

The Power of Habit

By Charles Duhigg. Taking you through case studies, showing examples and telling stories, Duhigg details the science behind our habits. In essence, *everything* we do is a result of some habit built up over time to relieve our minds from having to rethink life every day. I am still working on ways to make this practical to others, but personally, it has been absolutely eye-opening. I now (at least) notice what triggers my habits, and I am working to change some bad habits by changing my routines. This is an excellent book recommended by several inculencers. It should be right up at the top of your next reading list, it is that good.

Linchpin

By Seth Godin. *Linchpin* is more practical than *Tribes*, but tends along the same stylistic path. It takes a high-view approach to life, encouraging the reader to be and do the best he can. In essence, this book tells the reader to constantly give himself to grow, stretch himself, and do what he does best rather than getting caught in the common everyday tasks of life. In Christian terms, this translates to excellence in ministry and personally developing and working within your strongest spiritual gifts. And, if you are so inclined, taking everything you do up a level, motivating others around you to do the same.

How to Fail at Almost Everything and Still Win Big

By Dilbert creator Scott Adams. I did not realize how secular and profane Scott Adams was until I read this book. I was not anticipating the profanity. However, his unrelenting simplicity and optimism is both challenging and inspirational. What is more, he put more practical business concepts and personal time management principles into words than I have read in some whole books devoted to these topics! He is a unique writer and a good storyteller. He presents his points with such simplicity and clarity, you almost cannot disagree. Although he promotes some anti-God concepts as he pumps the humanistic agenda, he left me with more practical takeaways than I have received from a book in a long time. Recommended with reservations due to mild language every 30-40 pages.

Quiet

By Susan Cain. I watched a TED talk by Susan Cain on the topic of introverts and became immediately hooked. I bought the book immediately. I have always been fascinated by the topic of personalities, and I want to learn as much as possible about relating with people through their personalities. As an introvert myself, this book is encouraging to know that while we (in the author's terms) "live in an extrovert's world," the introverted person still can have a huge amount of influence if he chooses to leverage it. I recommend the book to introverted people to learn to work within their strengths, and I recommend it to extroverts in order to help them understand that shyness or quietness is not laziness, arrogance, weakness or lack of leadership.

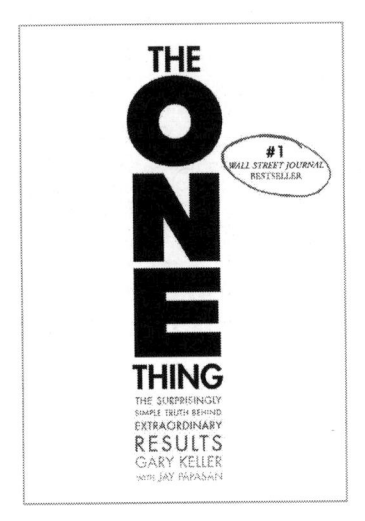

The One Thing

By Gary Keller and Jay Papasan. A podcast I listen to recommends this book a lot, but I found it somewhat dry and not as helpful as I had hoped. In my line of work and side-work, the ideals in this book are a bit out of reach, in that it encourages focus on essentially one major project at a time. In church work, I have little control over my schedule, sometimes, and my "One Thing" might change daily, at the whims of others' needs. Despite that, I found the book helpful. I learned about focusing on a project, ramming it out, and moving on to the next.

The Shallows

By Nicholas Carr. If you want to be depressed about your brain, read this book. However, if you also want to be mindful of how much you are being influenced—often without even realizing it—by your computer use, read this book. Pastor Wayne Hardy published an incredible follow-up article to this book in the technology issue of *The Global Baptist Times* publication. Highly recommended as a contemplative type of book rather than as a practical business book.

Simple Rules

By Don Sull. Although this book is not as highly rated as others on Amazon, I found it simple and helpful. Sure, it is a basic principle, overall, but the examples used in *Simple Rules* helped drive the point home that we can boil almost any big project or dream down to a few basic actions that we must take next. When we do the hard work of thinking about the basic rules, it makes anything big seem much smaller.

Business Principles

The Thank You Economy

By Gary Vaynerchuk. Yet another example of a secular book that preaches biblical principles. *The Thank You Economy* is a book about giving. Modern marketing strategies include giving of your expertise in any way that you can. It is said that the more you give, the more you are rewarded. As businesses and business leaders give of their time, their expertise and their knowledge, the market responds by rewarding them financially. This book teaches you to insert yourself into circles in which you can contribute, resulting in financial gain. We can learn to give as Christian leaders, too.

Platform

By Michael Hyatt. This book gives solid, practical tips on how to broaden your influence, especially in the social media realm. Michael Hyatt served as the CEO of a large publishing company, and later resigned to start his own company of writing, coaching and speaking on leadership principles. *Platform* was among his first written works after launching out on his own.

Will It Fly?

By Pat Flynn. This book takes you step by step through your next big idea to see whether it might have a large buy-in or not.

I should use this book, but I do not. I am usually the bone-head that gets wrapped up on an idea, spends the next three weeks doing it, and realizes later that no one cares about it. *Oh well*, I think. *At least it was fun to do*. Well, this is a book to help you NOT do that.

It is comprehensive in that it gives all the tools and step by step instructions on not only WHAT to do, but also HOW to do it. If you have a big idea you plan to launch, read this book first.

Finances

I am not a *fanatic* of Dave Ramsey's (like some people are), but I AM a *big fan*. I listen to his show, devour his Financial Peace University class materials and love him as a Christian public figure. I have worked through several of his resources, listed below:

Smart Money, Smart Kids

By Dave Ramsey and Rachel Cruze. Dave Ramsey produced a book and series of church and home lessons on raising kids to be wise with their current and future finances. This book is full of stories, tips, tricks and ideas on how to raise money-smart kids who are dedicated to giving, saving and spending their money for the glory of God.

Foundations in Personal Finance

By Dave Ramsey. The Dave Ramsey team has also created a high school and college finance program that I worked through at a Christian school. This curriculum is available for home study or in-school classrooms. It walks students through all the basics of finances and meets all national standards for education. Bible verses coincide with each chapter to show the biblical foundation on which these financial principles are built. Although it is not distinctly Christian (as it is adapted for public schools), the curriculum is a fabulous learning tool based on biblical principles.

The Millionaire Mind and The Millionaire Next Door

By Thomas Stanley. Recommended by Dave Ramsey, these books look at the disciplines of millionaires. It is a challenge to us as we learn to best budget the funds God gives us.

8. Websites

Bible Study

- I often consult free articles on <u>Bible.org</u> for background and other insights.
- I follow a daily reading plan on <u>Bible.com</u>.
- I often use <u>biblegateway.com</u> for quick formatting and link free copy/paste needs.

Christian Helps

CalvaryBaptist.pub

From the website: *Calvary Baptist Publications is a compilation of ministry resources originating from everyday church needs. Each book, booklet and minibook originated as a way to help our church—Calvary Baptist Church of Temecula, CA—and has since expanded to those beyond our local ministry.*

In the name, Calvary *denotes the Christian worldview from which every publication originates. Even non-ministry publications will be filtered through a Christ-honoring lens.* Baptist *emphasizes the stance and tone of the published material, immediately labeling the writing and aligning it with certain doctrines and practices. And* Publications, *well, it just seemed to fit. The logo encapsulates the ministry by hinting at both the cross and the book silhouettes. Calvary Baptist Publications exists to serve like-minded churches and Christians with simple resources that touch everyday life.*

RyanRench.com

As an associate pastor (or socio-pastor as a guy in my church says), I figure my life is all about creating content. Why not share it online, right? I hope to eventually expand the website to include more book reviews, sermon outlines, and other little youth and choir notes. For now, though, it is pretty bare-bones. If you subscribe to the email list, you'll receive a free e-book.

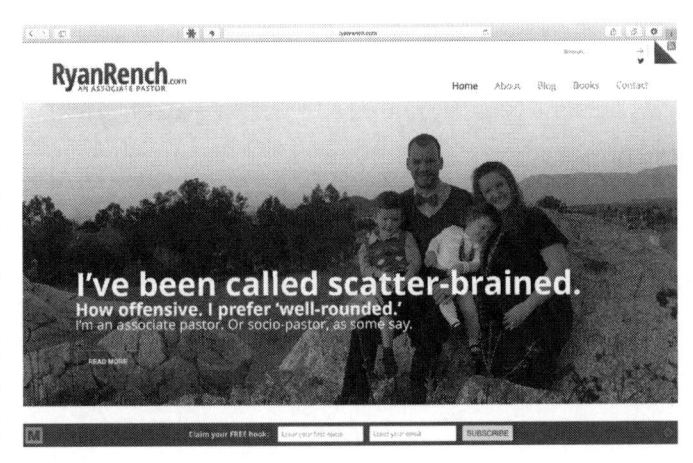

TheHeartlandConnect.com

In 2016, I became an officer of the alumni association of my college (Heartland Baptist Bible College in OKC). The Alumni Association launched a new platform called the Heartland Connect, which features content-rich articles to encourage ministry leaders. It features contributors of all types including pastors, associate pastors, their wives, and more.

Miscellaneous Favorites

SafeSmartSocial.com

I cannot remember how I stumbled onto Josh Ochs' website, but I started receiving quality reviews of every new app available to young people. Josh travels to schools and lectures on internet safety, warning young people to keep their online profile "light, bright and polite," warning them that colleges and employers are looking at young people's online habits when considering them for enrollment or a job. The website gives detailed warnings of what each app does, how kids are using it, and how parents can help their kids not get caught in the traps. This website is GREAT for youth pastors to review the apps without having to download and try each one.

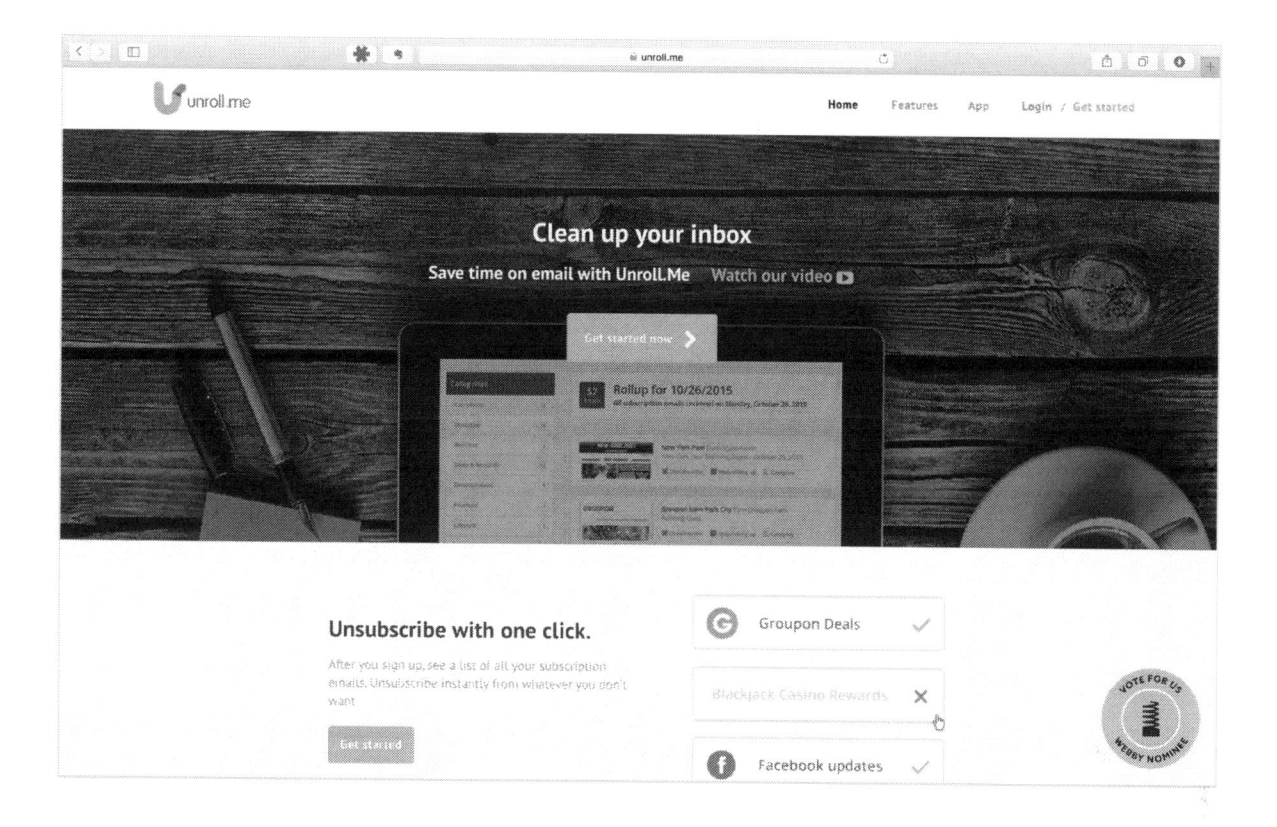

Unroll.Me

Visit Unroll.me or download their app to get started on all those random subscription emails you get throughout the day. I used Unroll.me to automatically unsubscribe me from over 300 newsletters, and "roll up" another 250 into a single daily roundup of about 30-50 emails. For the companies you DO want to hear from as soon as they send an email, you can leave it out of your rollup and it will be ignored by Unroll.me. There ARE some annoying things about it, like I cannot interact with the emails once I open them. Instead, I have to search for them in my Gmail archives. BUT, it is worth the clean inbox and the fact that I am not getting emails throughout my day.

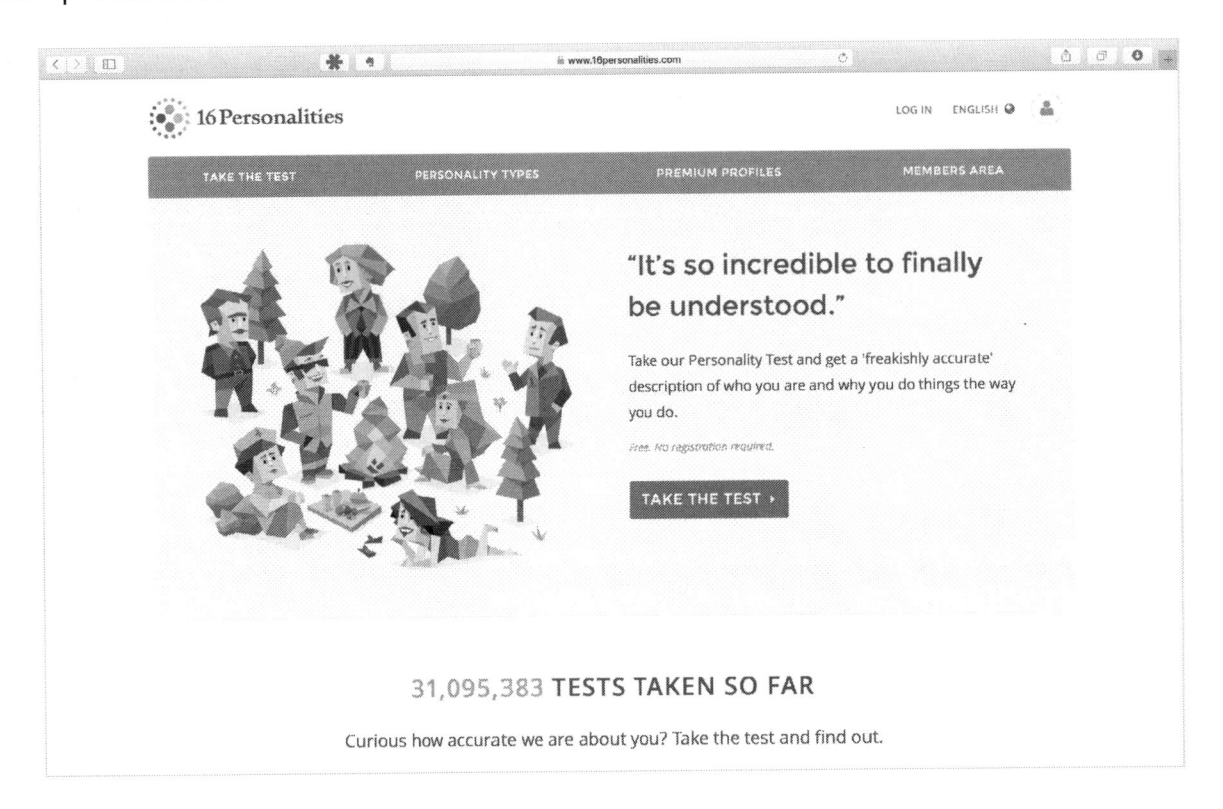

16Personalities.com

I have always tried to figure things out, including personalities. With all this banter today about being "open minded," a lot of it might start with understanding the other person's viewpoint. What makes him tick? What makes her think? What makes him argue? Why is she like that in a crowd? Knowing a person's personality helps. Knowing your OWN personality is huge, too.

It helps you account for your weaknesses. Although they will always be weaknesses, that does not mean you should ignore them, or "write them off" as inevitable. Hearing our weaknesses articulated should at least cause us to surround ourselves with those who are strong in those areas.

It helps you know where to maximize your time. On your strengths! We spend too much time propping up the areas God has made us bad at. We fret too much about being "not as good" at something as Mrs. Perfect over there. We compare ourselves too often. God says that is not good.

Instead, focus where you know God has strengthened you (by the way, that is not a psychology thing... that is a BIBLE thing – 1 Corinthians 12-14, Romans 12).

It helps you relate to others. When you know yourself and others better, you can find connections with almost anyone. *Love* might cover a multitude of sins, but so can *understanding*! When you love someone, you will seek to understand them better, even if they are strangers.

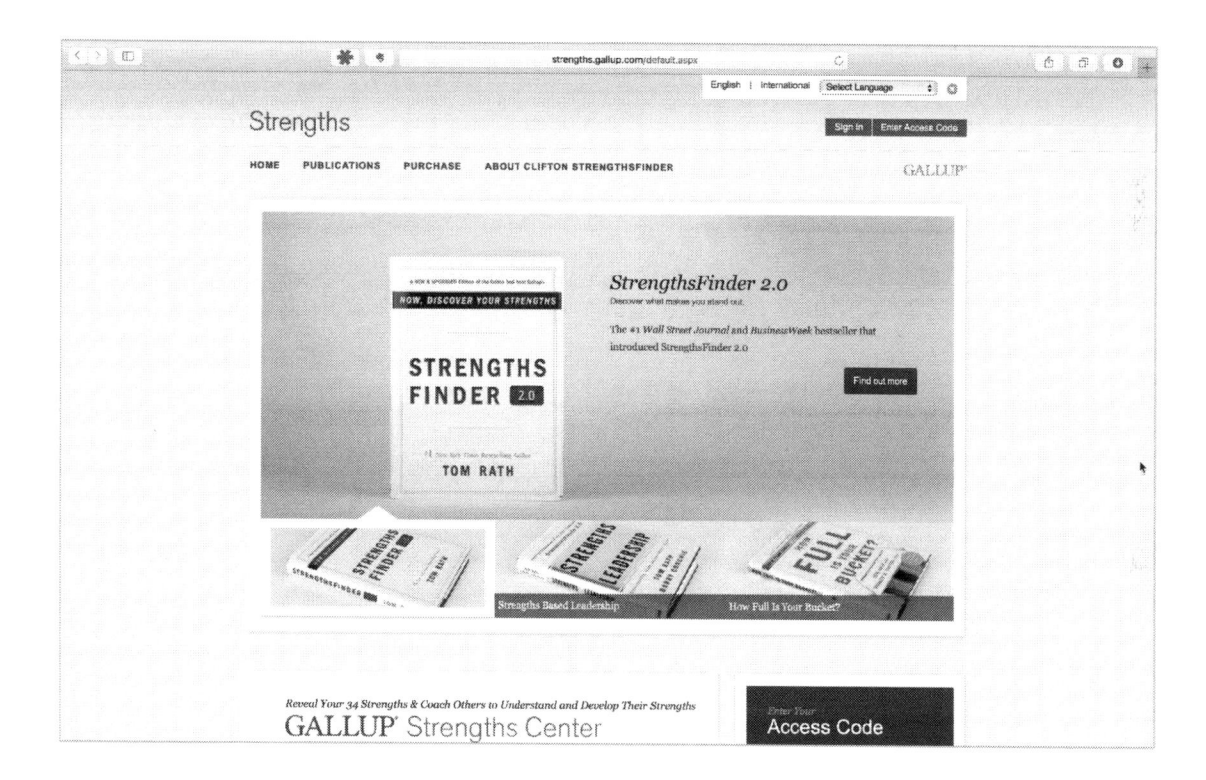

StrengthFinder.com

Related to a personality test is a new form of test called the Strengths Finder Test. You answer personal questions as you would any other test, but these questions are structured to find what you are best at. The Strengths Test app lists your top five strengths in order.

They include out of the ordinary categories (ones I had never seen, at least) such as adaptability, arranger, achiever, connectedness, command, focus, includes, input, strategic, significance, or woo, for example. I had NO idea these were even classifications, but when I took the test, I was pleasantly surprised to see not only how *accurate* it was, but how *revealing* it was.

Before taking the test, I thought I had a good idea of what my top 5 strengths would be.

I was wrong. What I thought was top, was nearer to 4 or 5, and other traits took my top spots (learner, analytical, strategic).

Since then, I see my strengths (learning and analyzing) in almost *everything* I do, whereas in the past I might have leaned more toward achieving (my #4).

Note: forgive me for using myself as the example. I wanted to show that there are NO right/wrong answers. The point is to strengthen your strengths. Now, for example, I feed my "learning" strength more than anything else, and have used the past couple years to take in more information than ever before.

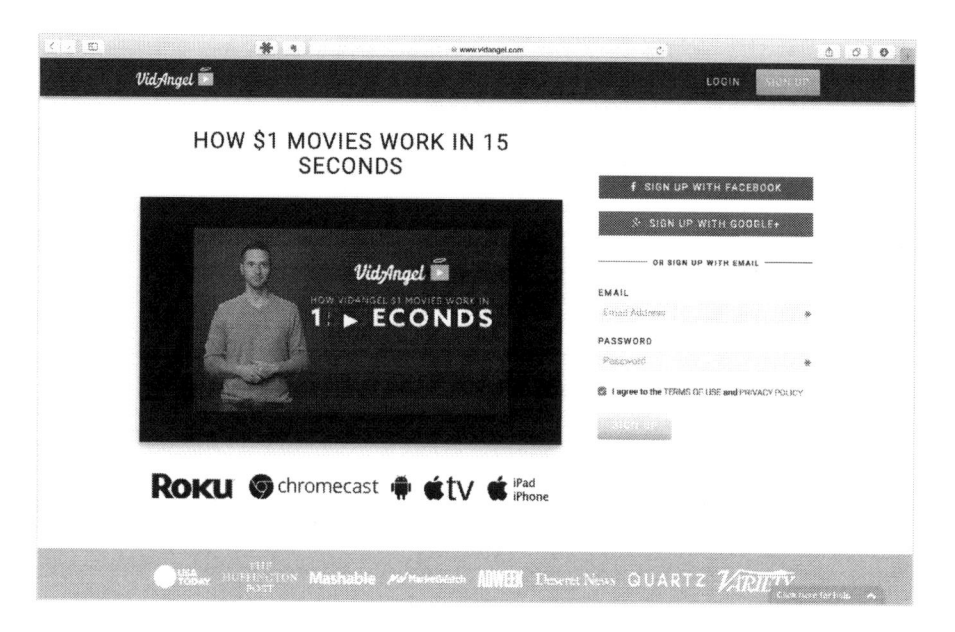

VidAngel.com

A lot of TV filtering services have come and gone, but VidAngel is my latest favorite. There is no hardware to buy, no filters to download onto a thumb drive, no DVDs to order and wait for shipping, and no hassle. It is all streamed video that you set the filters for whenever you want (mid-movie, if you desire). VidAngel filters visual and audio, including every level of immodesty, nudity, or even kissing. You can remove suggestive jokes, crude humor, and all expletives.

You purchase your first movie for $20 (then you own it, so you can legally edit it and watch it for home use), watch it, and sell it back to VidAngel for $19 credit. Essentially, it is a $1 filtered rental. Technically, it is a purchase and return. It has been a fun way to watch some action and adventure movies that we might not have otherwise watched if we could not clean them up. One obvious warning: do not go around quoting your "new favorite movie" as a preaching illustration. You might get some wide eyes from the kids who watched the NON-edited version!

(P.S. I get a little one-time discount on my account and YOU get a $19 credit if you sign up by going to RyanRench.com/vidangel)

9. Podcasts

I Listen Regularly to:

Youth Ministry Life

This podcast was started by a few youth pastor friends of mine. They interview guests on topics like pornography, Bible study, creativity, technology, and hosting big days; and give their own experiences from working in their respective churches. I love the podcast because of its humor; oh... and its content is good, too!

Story Grid

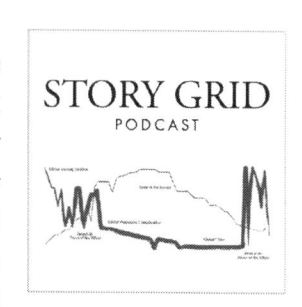

If you are into writing (particularly fiction), start from episode one of the Story Grid Podcast and binge-listen. I did that, and something about the first few episodes intrigued me so much that I have listened to almost every episode so far. I will be honest... it took me a few episodes before I barely started to grasp the structure (it is a LOT to take in), but now, it has changed the way I read books, watch movies, and think of stories. Shawn Coyne is an editor and author with decades of experience, condensing all he has learned into this format he calls the Story Grid, which he uses with authors to show what works and what does not work in telling stories. The podcast host (Tim Grahl) is a little drab, but Shawn in remarkable (I love experts).

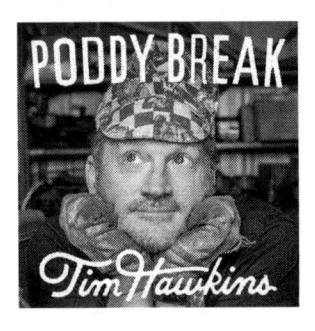

Poddy Break

By comedian Tim Hawkins. As a professional comedian, Tim Hawkins is inherently entertaining, but surprisingly insightful, as well. I do not subscribe to all his theology, but I like his positive worldview, and I have learned a lot about stage presence and humor, and have been introduced to a few other clean comics whom he features. Plus, his teenage son does a "spoiled rich kid" character that is as good as Tim.

Smart Passive Income

By Pat Flynn. In 2011, I clicked on the icon promoting this podcast and listened to a squirrelly voiced guy talk about online businesses. I had been building websites on the side for a couple years and was always interested in tips and tricks to improve my work, so I clicked through to his website. At the top right was a number with a dollar sign. $50,000. *Wow! That's a lot of money online,* I thought. *Wait, what?! That was last MONTH's income report, not last YEAR's.*

Each month since then (a few years ago), his income has increased, and he now consistently makes 2 or 3 times that each month. The podcast features interviews with other entrepreneurs who share tips and stories from their companies, and I always learn a nugget of info that helps me keep building something.

The Idea Talks

Hosted by Steven Miller with Pastor Josh Teis of Southern Hills Baptist Church. Every month, these men bring in a guest to discuss various ministry topics. The podcast episode on prayer, for example, featured interviews of two pastors with unique approaches to corporate prayer in their churches.

Dave Ramsey Show

This is an oldie but goody. All three hours of the Dave Ramsey Show are now uploaded as a free podcast. In addition, DaveRamsey.com and the Dave Ramsey Show app can stream the show for free. Dave Ramsey offers money advice based on biblical principles.

Andy Stanley Leadership

No, I do not like his stance on the Bible: "Stop saying, 'the Bible says...'" No, I do not like his stance on small churches, "If you go to a small church, you're so stinkin' selfish..." No, I do not like that he avoids the deep sinfulness of homosexuality, "It was plain old adultery [a church leader's divorce and homosexual affair with another man]." But I could give reasons for NOT liking a lot of authors I read after. However, I have found the leadership principles from this podcast immediately applicable. The podcast gives stories of company turnarounds (like Home Depot) or pithy aphorisms that stick with you like, "Make it better." I do not recommend the podcast for its theology, but for its practicality.

Thom Rainer On Leadership

In his down-to-earth Southern style, Thom Rainer talks about all things ministry. With a few decades of ministry experience in Southern Baptist churches and now as CEO of Lifeway Resources, Dr. Rainer gives practical advice on everyday church topics including follow-up visits, guest cards, church twitter accounts, staff compensation, ministry spouses, and more.

I Listen Occasionally to:

This Is Your Life

By Michael Hyatt. If I see an episode title that looks interesting to me, I will download the episode and listen. I have read a few of Michael Hyatt's books and I follow his blog, but I do not find as much of a connection with him as I do with some other authors. He gives quick tips and tools that are often helpful. Those are the episodes I gravitate towards.

ChurchMag Podcast

I follow their blog and occasionally click through to their podcast. They present tech ideas and tools such as website optimizations, online giving solutions and more. They have a good staff, but I have not fully bought into their style.

EntreLeadership

By Dave Ramsey. I enjoyed the book *EntreLeadership* by Dave Ramsey, and the follow-up podcast hosts other leaders and entrepreneurs who are doing quality work. The host asks insightful questions and the guests always deliver value from their journeys through entrepreneurship.

The Tech Guy

With Leo Laporte. Long-time radio host Leo Laporte hosts several podcasts on all things tech. He has an easy-going voice that makes techy things sound simple, and I listen to this podcast maybe once every two months as a filler.

48 Days to the Work You Love

With Dan Miller. Dave Ramsey often recommends Dan Miller's book and podcast about finding or creating a job. Dan answers listener's pre-recorded questions about starting businesses, increasing their income, managing their time and more practical topics. The podcast is encouraging and useful for generating extra ideas.

10. Various Ministry Ideas

The following article shows how unfocused a "miscellaneous" category can be.

Focus... Is It a Dirty Word in Ministry?

For an associate pastor, focus might seem impossible.

If I have learned anything over the past few years, it is that I am scatterbrained and cannot focus. Thanks to a "strength cards" activity we did and the leader calling pity upon me (literally, "If anyone has a topic from every category, I feel bad for you...") Yep, that was me.

The activity started with 100 examples of topics that either interested us or not (preaching, sewing, drawing, analytical thinking, etc.), and we categorized ourselves into two piles: "yes, that's me," or, "No, that's not me." Starting the round with high 70's of "Yes, that's me" cards and whittling eventually through the process down to 10 was painful... poor me.

The Strengths Finder cards activity helped me, though. I WAS scatterbrained. I still am, but at least I know it, now. I used to think of myself as well-versed in many different things. I used to think I was superman! Now I realize I can do a lot of things, but cannot do any of them well.

However, as an associate pastor, I am more than a youth pastor. I sincerely believe God has gifted me as He sees fit, and I am doing my best to try to focus on the most important things in my life, rather than *all* the things in my life.

I am interested in several things: Bible study, technology, writing, teaching, preaching, graphics/web, people development, family, music, construction, business and much, much more. But I cannot do all of my hobbies and passions every week. I need to learn to sprint. Meaning, I need to learn to focus on one thing for a short project, and then move on to the next sprint.

For me, it is a curse—I get bored with one task or project when I do it repeatedly, so I toy with new things that will push me further. The upside is that people like me are driven. The downside is that things can tend to get neglected over time.

So, I work to focus on ONE thing while at the same time being responsible for (and interested in) MANY things.

How do we as associate pastors reconcile all the demands on our time without ALL the areas suffering for it? If you figure it out, let me know!

Lesson Notes

Finance Sermon

Leading up to our church's Stewardship Sunday, our teens and adults combined during our regular Sunday School hour for a four-week financial wisdom series taught by men from our church. This was the lesson I taught:

CHURCH HANDOUT

All month leading up to our Stewardship Sunday we have heard God's perspective on money: how to get it, how not to get it, how to give it, how to save it, and how to spend it. We have learned that the topic of money is important to God, so it should be stewarded well.

When we think of our lives as though we are not the owner, it changes everything. It is a criminal offense for, say, a mutual fund manager to use the money he's managing to buy himself a nice house! Likewise, to use *our* money (and our lives!) as though WE are the owners is robbery, according to Malachi.

So when we use God's money, we should be especially careful about *how* we use it. The men in the previous weeks have done a great job showing us God's thoughts from His Word.

Today, we wrap up the 4-week series with fewer Bible verses (although these are biblical principles) but a few tips and tools of financial basics. The most basic categories of all are INCOMING and OUTGOING:

INCOMING

There are a few ways to get money coming in: taxes, stealing (is that the same?), welfare, and w_____. [work] Do the last one.

A few months ago, I gave these tips to the Teens of Faith. Maybe boosting your income involves the following ideas:

- Work extra jobs
- Get more education: online college, read books, listen to courses or podcasts, research new ideas online

JOB IDEAS:

- Window cleaning – door to door or businesses. $30 startup costs.
- Baby sitting – Dave Ramsey's daughter – resume, case studies, full report on why she would be the most dependable
- Curb painting
- Lawn mowing
    - Advertise. Make signs and handouts. Pass them around your neighborhood – ask the old ladies in your street if you can do any weeding for them.
    - And then give them tracts ☺
- Sell stuff on EBay – junk around the house, garage sales, etc.
- Teaching yourself graphic or web design – stick a sign in your yard.
- Pet cleanup services – making rounds every other day for $5/week (or $3/week for one day). Stack up clients and carry a bucket and shovel around. Offer discounts for multiple animals. Include cat litter changing, too. Search online for other services similar.
- Hanging flyers on doors
- Washing cobwebs off houses
- Menu planning service
- Grocery delivery – if you live within walking distance of a store
- Dog-walking
- Garage sale/cleaning help – advertise yourself
- Crochet animals and sell them on Etsy or eBay

OUTGOING

To accomplish this section, you have to know what is happening with your money. A budget is not a bad thing—it's a way to know what's happening. It can be low tech (all cash), mid, or high tech (all online).

G_____ [Give]

The tithe (10%) comes first, then you budget the rest. In the Scripture, the word *giving* is always *in addition to* the tithe (i.e. the stewardship commitment, missions, Easter offering, etc. are above the tithe. I know a pastor who tithes 10% and gives an additional 20% to missions.)

S_____ [Save]

Know SHORT term and LONG term needs. Do not let summer camp or Christmas surprise you (short term); and plan for new roofs, new AC units, new cars and retirement (long term).

S_____ [Spend]

My favorite section! USE the money God has given you! You're allowed to use it on yourself and your family. ☺ My family uses both online spending (for bills) and the cash system for everything else: grocery, fast food, restaurants, gifts, amusement, Ryan spendingn(my favorite), and Jamie spending. When the cash runs out, we wait until next month!

TOOLS

Budget: Mint.com, EveryDollar app, Cash system – lazy man's way! ☺

Books: *Smart Money, Smart Kids*; *My Total Money Makeover*; *The Millionaire Next Door*

TEACHING NOTES

The following section is my preaching notes from the lesson I taught on finance. It corresponds to the handout copied above.

These other guys with their credentials:

- LONG careers and plenty of good financial choices
- Years of faithful giving

They did a GOOD job laying out all the biblical perspectives.

Today is some practical application of those principles.

- Me?? A kid who grew up learning to work
- Hank – taught me the blessings of money
- If you have the capacity to work with a kid in church, or the neighborhood, do it.
- Creates an appetite for WORK.

Studied this stuff

- Through high school
    - Worked
    - Bought a $1000 guitar
    - $2400 truck
    - Paid for college
- In college
    - found some Dave Ramsey MP3s
    - listened 3x through his course
- Dave Ramsey fan, not a fanatic, but like his stuff (using it)
- I am NO pro, especially if THESE guys said they were no pros.
- Seems like their principles are GOOD.

[SEE HANDOUT – "INCOMING" SECTION]

RESOURCES:

PODCASTS:

App on my phone

- Hour long radio shows, essentially
- They're recorded
- When THEY create the show,
- It alerts ME that a new show is available
- I can listen ANY time
- And SKIP the commercials! Love that.

Dave Ramsey Show podcast

48 Days To the Work You Love podcast and book by Dan Miller (Christian author)

START book by Jon Acuff (Christian)

Three basics that Dave Ramsey teaches kids with (we can ALL learn from these)

GIVE, SAVE, SPEND

> These are the OUTGOING

GIVE

- I start here, because it kind of skips the budget.
- Off the top
- Covered that in previous lessons
- Tithe – 10% off top

Giving is ABOVE the tithe

- Stewardship
- Missions
- Easter offering

BUDGET

- The rest, we budget
- NOT a bad work

- I LIKE that word!
- Helps me know what I can spend!

Low, mid, high tech

- Paper/pen
- Apps and online only
- We do a fusion of both

List INCOME

- Combined
- Everything

List EXPENSES

- All bills
- Upcoming stuff
- Include SAVING
- Subtract to equal ZERO

Example: Here's what WE do:

- Fusion of high and low tech

INCOMING:

- All online
- Tracked through mint.com (free)
- Linked bank accounts
- To me, the security is as good or better than low tech, so I have NO fears
- Direct deposit
- Amazon sales
- EBay sales through PayPal
- Book sales

- Our jobs here at church
- Paid in check? Chase app on phone: Immediately deposited online.
- All online
- So we KNOW how much we have coming in. Regular income each month

OUTGOING

- A couple HIGH TECH – online savings
- BIG purchases – annual renewals, saving for car, etc.
- ONLINE payments like BILLS

High tech are the regular ones that we could not necessarily save money on anyway. We do:

- Mortgage
- Gas
- Phone
- Auto, life ins.
- Utilities

I will throw this in here:

SAVING (Blank on sheet)

- Budgeting means planning your saving.
- That's so basic, but some people panic because they FORGET that
- Summer camp is in the summer this year! Wait, we just started 2016, right? No? It's MAY already?!
- And Christmas is in December!
- SHORT term – within a year or two
- LONG term – varying: 2 yrs. to retirement!
- So a long time ago, we figured up how much we'd need for each thing we are saving for, and we divided by 12 to know how much PER MONTH to put in
    - Life insurance
    - Dental

- Vacation – covered a lot with my little side incomes
- Christmas
- Home improve
- Auto repair
- Auto upgrade
- Retirement

THINK
- I think the TAKEAWAY is not the specifics
- It's this: THINK.
- KNOW what's coming
- And plan accordingly
- I love what one of the teen ladies did a few years ago
    - Knowing that camp was coming up
    - Down payment needed
    - Told us: "I have been saving $5/mo. since camp last year to get by down payment!"
    - She had it!

I do not mind helping people, but it bothers me when people will not cover a $50 down payment when I hear about:

- Edwards Cinema
- Do not go to movies, so I did not know the prices
- $11.75 adults
- $9 child
- Starbucks
- Wife's favorite:
- White chocolate mocha with raspberry
- $4.95 just looked it up

So we try to save up for big stuff AND little stuff

- New suit
- IPhone upgrades

- New iPad
- So WE do our SAVING mostly with the HIGH TECH option

But the THIRD BLANK there is SPENDING

- This is the OTHER part of your budget
- MY favorite part!
- Because a budget is not LIMITING
- It's FREE-ING
- I know how much I am allowed to spend
- And if I need more
- I have got to earn it!
- So our SPENDING is done mostly low-tech

Went to CASH last year – lazy man's way!

- Do not have to do math, just look in the slot to see if we have money.
- Love it a lot more
- My parents have always done cash
- We did it because it's hard to keep track of SO many transactions
- So we ignore most of the small ones by using cash
- Jamie pulls a certain amount each month
- Organizes in our little container
- Spends ONLY what's in that container!
- When the money runs out, we wait till next month.
- I LOVE new months!
- I get $10 spending money
- Jamie gets the rest! ☺
- Money runs out, we are done
- Giving my wife a hard time about our bare cupboards right now
- Ran out of fruit snacks last week when mom was at the ladies retreat!
- And apples!
- And bananas!

- And all the pleasantries that my kids enjoy!
- Left me with NOTHING!
- Haha!
- Used up the last frozen pizza
- Tragedy of the world!
- She said, "End of the month"

Just being open and honest with you, for some specific ideas. We do:

- $_____ grocery
- $20 fast food
- $10 ministry food
- $30 restaurants
- $15 gift
- $15 amusement
- $10 Ryan
- $10 Jamie
- When the money runs out, we have to wait till next month.
- Obviously, we push the limits sometimes
- "Eh… how much do we have in…"

TOOLS (see handout)

TIPS

- WORK to make good money. America is still the land of opportunity. There is plenty of money to be made.
- GIVE off the top. Then do your budget.
- SAVE an emergency fund. Start with $1000 to bail you out of little things, then get out of debt.
- ELIMINATE debt. All of it as fast as you can. Do not spend what you do not have.
- KNOW what you're spending. Call it budgeting, tracking, or whatever-ing. Know that a weekly $7 Starbucks run costs $28/mo. or $350/year!

- SAVE a bigger emergency fund (after debt is eliminated). If you lost your job and had $0 income, save enough money to live on for at least 3 months.
- SAVE for big purchases. Cars, house upgrades, kids' college, retirement.
- PLAN for the future. Think about your goals and plan now how to get there: invest in mutual funds or pay off your house, for example.

Conclusion: "I already DO all this! I did not learn anything this month!"

- First, I am leery of people that say they did not learn *anything*.
- That's either arrogant, or forgetful, or unobservant, or unteachable, or something! But none of them are good!
- Nuggets – if you pick up on ONE thing, GOOD!
- Even if you're ONLY reminded, let it ENCOURAGE you that you're on the right track
- The REASON we plan our money – where we started this morning – being good STEWARDS
- God is the owner, so it's our duty (obligation?) to use our money well. For Him.

Co-Op "Catechism" Class

On Thursday mornings, a small group of homeschooled kids and teens meet at our church for classes and activities. Our chapel time consists of a recurring curriculum which works through several major Bible doctrines. We approach it similar to a catechism, using rote learning through question/answer format, adding one new aspect each week. Since the students range from Kindergarten to high school, the lessons are basic yet theologically sound. Following, you will see our weekly handout with questions and memory verses:

Doctrine

What is doctrine? The teachings of the Bible.

1 Timothy 4:16 **Take heed unto thyself, and unto the doctrine**; *continue in them: for in doing this thou shalt both save thyself, and them that hear thee.*

God's Word

What is the Bible? The Bible is God's Word.

1 Peter 1:21 For the prophecy came not in old time by the will of man: but **holy men of God spake as they were moved by the Holy Ghost.**

Theology (The Study of God)

Who/what is God? God is a spirit.

John 4:24 **God is a spirit**: *and they that worship him must worship him in spirit and in truth.*

How do we know there's a God? Through creation and His Word.

Psalm 19:1-6 **The heavens declare the glory of God**...

Romans 1:18-32

John 1:1 In the beginning was the Word, and the Word was with God, and the Word was God.

How can we know God? Know Jesus Christ.

John 4:6-7 Jesus saith unto him, I am the way, the truth, and the life: no man cometh unto the Father, but by me. ⁷ **If ye had known me, ye should have known my Father also**: *and from henceforth ye know him, and have seen him.*

Pneumatology (The Study of the Holy Spirit)

Who/what is the Holy Spirit? The Holy Spirit is God.

1 John 5:7 For there are three that bear record in heaven, the Father, the Word, and the Holy Ghost: and **these three are one.**

Our Enemy (Satan)

Who/what is the Satan? Satan was an angel. He turned against God and is now the leader of God's enemies.

1 Peter 5:8 Be sober, be vigilant; because your **adversary the devil**, *as a roaring lion, walketh about, seeking whom he may devour:*

Our Beginnings

Where did we come from? Everything was created by God.

Genesis 1:1 In the beginning God created the heaven and the earth.

Our Problem (Hamartiology: the study of sin)

Is anyone good enough to get to heaven? No. We have sinned.

Romans 3:10 As it is written, **There is none righteous, no, not one:**

Romans 3:23 For all have sinned, and come short of the glory of God;

Why are we sinners? We are born in sin.

Romans 5:12 **Wherefore,** *as by one man sin entered into the world, and death by sin; and* **so death passed upon all men, for that all have sinned***:*

Our Saviour (Christology)

Who is Jesus? Jesus is God's son, born of a virgin.

Isaiah 7:14 Therefore the Lord himself shall give you a sign; Behold, a virgin shall conceive, and bear a son, and shall call his name Immanuel.

John 1:14 **And the Word was made flesh, and dwelt among us...**

Galatians 4:4 ...God sent forth his son, made of a woman...

Our Salvation (Soteriology)

What Did Jesus say? "...ye must be born again."

John 3:3, 7 Jesus answered and said unto him, Verily, verily, I say unto thee, Except a man be born again, he cannot see the kingdom of God... Marvel not that I said unto thee, **Ye must be born again.**

What does *born again* mean? Being saved.

John 3:16 **For God so loved the world, that he gave his only begotten Son, that whosoever believeth in him should not perish, but have everlasting life.**

Who can be saved? Anyone who repents and places their faith in Jesus.

Romans 10:13 **For whosoever shall call upon the name of the Lord shall be saved.**

What is repentance? Turning from sin to Christ.

Acts 20:21 Testifying both to the Jews, and also to the Greeks, **repentance toward God, and faith toward our Lord Jesus Christ.**

Our Church (Ecclesiology)

What is a church? A called-out assembly of Christians.

The Greek word "ecclesia" (translated as "church") is a 2-part word: <u>Ek</u> *– "out of"; and* <u>Klesis</u> *– "a calling." The word "Church" means "a called out assembly," and is used by Christians primarily.*

What does it mean to be Baptist? Use this acrostic:

Biblical authority—we follow what the Bible says. 2 Tim. 3:16

Autonomy of the local church—no one rules us from outside. Matthew 18:17, Acts 1:15-26, 13:1-3

Priesthood of the believer—every Christian can talk straight to God. 1 Pet. 2:5

Two offices, Pastor and deacon—not cardinal, pope, priest or anything else. Ephesians 4:11, 1 Tim. 3:1-13

Individual soul liberty—you choose your eternity. Gal. 5:1

Saved, baptized church membership—we want the church to stay pure. Acts 2:27-42

Two ordinances, baptism and the Lords Supper—not foot washing. These keep the church pure. 1 Corinthians 11:2, Acts 2:41-42; 1 Corinthians 11:23-34

Separation of church and state—neither controls the other. Matthew 22:15-22; 28:18-20; Romans 13:1-7

Our Security

Can I lose my salvation? No. We are kept by God's power.

*1 Peter 1:5 **Who are kept by the power of God through faith unto salvation** ready to be revealed in the last time.*

*Romans 8:38-39 For I am persuaded, that neither death, nor life, nor angels, nor principalities, nor powers, nor things present, nor things to come, 39. Nor height, nor depth, **nor any other creature, shall be able to separate us from the love of God**, which is in Christ Jesus our Lord.*

*Romans 6:23 For the wages of sin is death, but **the gift of God is <u>eternal life</u> through Jesus Christ our Lord.***

Salvation's Change in Christians

How many types of people are there? Two. The righteous and the wicked.

*Romans 3:10 **As it is written, There is none righteous, no, not one:***

How can I be righteous? By being saved.

*Romans 3:22 **Even the righteousness of God which is by faith of Jesus Christ unto all** and upon all them that believe: for there is no difference:*

The Government

What's the government's job? To serve and protect.

*Romans 13:4 **For he is the minister of God to thee for good**. But if thou do that which is evil, be afraid; for he beareth not the sword in vain: for he is the minister of God, a revenger to execute wrath upon him that doeth evil.*

What's our duty to the government? To support and be subject to them.

*Romans 13: 5-6 **Wherefore ye must needs be subject**, not only for wrath, but also for conscience sake. 6 For for this cause **pay ye tribute also**: for they are God's ministers, attending continually upon this very thing.*

End Times (Eschatology)

What's happens next in the world? The return of the resurrected Jesus Christ.

*Acts 1:11 Which also said, Ye men of Galilee, why stand ye gazing up into heaven? **this same Jesus, which is taken up from you into heaven, shall so come in like manner** as ye have seen him go into heaven.*

How will Jesus return? In the clouds.

*1 Thessalonians 4:16-17 For the Lord himself shall descend from heaven with a shout, with the voice of the archangel, and with the trump of God: and **the dead in Christ shall rise first: 17 Then we which are alive and remain shall be caught up together with them in the clouds**, to meet the Lord in the air: and so shall we ever be with the Lord.*

What will Jesus do? Rule and reign the earth for 1,000 years.

Rev. 20:1-1

Ministry Tools

Throwable Microphone

I saw an idea on getcatchbox.com and worked to duplicate it.

- **Design.** *Their* throwable microphone has a nice handle and plush sides.
- **Color.** *Their* throwable microphone comes with a variety of color options.
- **Sensors.** *Their* throwable microphone has built-in sensors that sense when it is being thrown and caught.
- **Cost.** *Their* throwable microphone is $549.

I propose *my* version:

- **Design**. Wrap a church wireless lapel mic in foam padding. A precut form such as the box from Apple's Magic Mouse (that is what I used) should work perfectly.
- **Color.** Customizable at no additional cost! Purchase beautifully colored and artistically vibrant duct tape (any major super-store). Wrap foam cube carefully. Craft a sweet duct tape handle.
- **Sensors**? Yes! (Sound man at the back hitting the "mute" button when thrown)
- **Cost.** $549? NO! On sale today! For the price on one roll of duct tape and some foam, you can build your own throwable microphone today!

Apple TV

I had our intern do the research, purchase the materials, install the TV, and run the network cable through the attic for the internet connection. Here are some ideas of what we have used it for:

- Weekly – Flickr slideshow and college group music

- Wednesday night video lesson series
- Boggle app game
- Showed special Ken Ham/Bill Nye debate
- Lesson notes
- "Mirror" of the teens while they are singing
- YouTube skits in preparation for comedy night
- Show pictures of youth pastor's newborn babies
- Fat pics air played before class ("Fatbooth" app. See pictures below)

Digital Encouragement File

I have always saved the hand-written letters that I have received from people, but I have never stored my encouraging texts. After receiving several encouraging text messages from teens and parents, rather than letting the texts get lost in my memory, I copied them to a new list on my phone called "Encouragements."

I put the date, the sender, and the message, and I add a little context to why they sent it. If I receive an encouraging email, in my Gmail, I have an "encouraging" label that I apply.

Interns

Summer 2013, was the first time we ever had interns. A Freshman and a Junior from Heartland Baptist Bible College in Oklahoma City came to work for 12 weeks at our church last summer while we housed, fed and trained them; and paid their down payment for the next semester of college. Since then, we have had two interns per summer.

Our two summer interns do everything for us. I mean, everything! They run the bus ministry, oversee outreach, prep for Sundays, run fundraisers, organize church functions, go to camp, make videos, renovate the youth room, organize youth activities... everything!

I start many mornings with the interns, training and helping them. We look over what they accomplished since the last time we met and we plan out what they are going to do next. This fosters communication and friendship. They preach several times to the teens and give announcements in church to help them gain valuable experience.

Ministry. Their main ministry is with the teens. We use the whole summer as a beneficial time for both the interns and the teens.

Youth Activities. The interns help set up and run youth activities. They gain valuable experience in running, promoting, gathering materials for and witnessing the overall process happen from the leaders' side of things.

Youth Fundraisers. We conduct our annual yard sale and the interns to help gather donations, price the items, hang signage and sell the items. They were able to witness a youth group raise over $4,000 for a couple weeks' work.

Preaching. Each intern is able to preach a 3-week mini-series on Wednesday nights. Rather than focus on a one-off sermon, I work with them to develop an idea that might spread across more than one message. After each time they preach, we meet the next day in my office and critique the structure and delivery of the message.

Modeling. More than what they DO for the teens, the interns make an impact in who they ARE as Christians. It is always great for the teens to see two normal, cool, young, energetic, fun-loving, goofy guys who are also passionate about the Lord, fervent in their prayer, love preaching, love serving and love people. Our interns are young—close to the age of the teens—but they model the maturity and excitement that comes from serving the Lord with youthful energy.

Respect. Because of the interns' youth, we intentionally encourage the teens to refer to the interns by a "Brother" title. While the interns in themselves do nothing to earn the respect of a title, we teach the teens to respect *the position*. It is not the *person* we are respecting but the position. Further, the respect that *I* choose to show someone is *my* choice... not his. It is not in what *they* want to be called—it is the level of respect that *I* want to show them.

Fun. The interns earn a lot of respect over the summer, but they do it by playing with the teens. A wonderful part of having them on youth staff is to help liven up the group. I can tend to be "all business" and come across quite firm through the preaching, so I balance myself on youth staff with the fun-loving interns. The teens love them, and the interns make it easy to connect with more teens. The interns are my eyes and ears for certain areas I personally need to work on, and I use their input in things I do day by day.

If you can get a couple knuckleheads to give up their summer at your church, I would recommend it. Run them ragged and then send them back to college!

Interning Well. After several summers of interns, I compiled a list of articles into a 175-page book that new interns now read before summer. This book includes things that each intern must know, including step by step instructions on certain ministries, our church's philosophies, work ethics articles and much more. When an intern received training in our intern staff meetings, the training time would be followed up with a written article on the topic and eventually became the book *Interning Well*, available on Amazon.com by Calvary Baptist Publications. More info at CalvaryBaptist.pub.

11. Other Random Stuff

Medi-Share

A few Christian companies now offer healthcare alternatives. Financial services like MediShare are clear to say that they are NOT insurance, but they cover ALL medical bills.

Here's how it works:

- Christians sign up and pay monthly dues
- When a medical bill comes up, members submit their bill to the sharing company
- The sharing company publishes the bill to all members
- The medical bill is paid from the shared funds

In essence, each member is paying their medical bills with cash rather than billing an insurance company. Many doctors and hospitals charge less when a person is self-insured.

Medi-Share Program Options

Annual Household Portion	$500	$1,250	$2,500	$3,750	$5,000	$7,500	$10,000
Standard Monthly Share	N/A	$616.00	$498.00	$397.00	$338.00	$242.00	$174.00
Healthy Monthly Share	N/A	$492.00	$398.00	$318.00	$271.00	$195.00	$139.00

Conditions apply. Please read below for details.

Each member is responsible for an "Annual Household Portion" (the MAX amount they will pay out in a year). After their AHP is paid, anything ABOVE that amount is paid in full by Medi-Share shared funds.

Members can agree to pay up to $10,000 as their AHP, or as little as $1,250. The table above shows the monthly rates for 3+ people, with the oldest member being 30 years old, as an example. Depending on the AHP (think of it as an annual out-of-pocket deductible), rates are extremely affordable compared to current healthcare prices (our church was paying around $2500/mo. for two families—my parents and my family).

I have an HSA (Health Savings Account) at a bank, allowing me to save and spend money on health related purchases tax-free. The amount that the church WAS paying now goes into my HSA (max $10k/yr. per family) to use as my AHP. That means, healthy people who never go to the doctor can save up to $10k/year in another tax sheltered account, which can later be rolled into an IRA if it is not used.

Medi-Share has great rates, great payouts and great customer service. They are professional and informational.

If you DO sign up, please mention my name (Ryan Rench) as the referral. It will give our church a small bonus. Other companies like Samaritans Purse are doing similar things. Do some research and you will be pleased!

FBA – Fulfillment by Amazon

I earn a few thousand dollars a year by buying stuff at thrift stores and selling them on Amazon.com. Anyone can do it pretty easily with "Fulfillment by Amazon," or FBA.

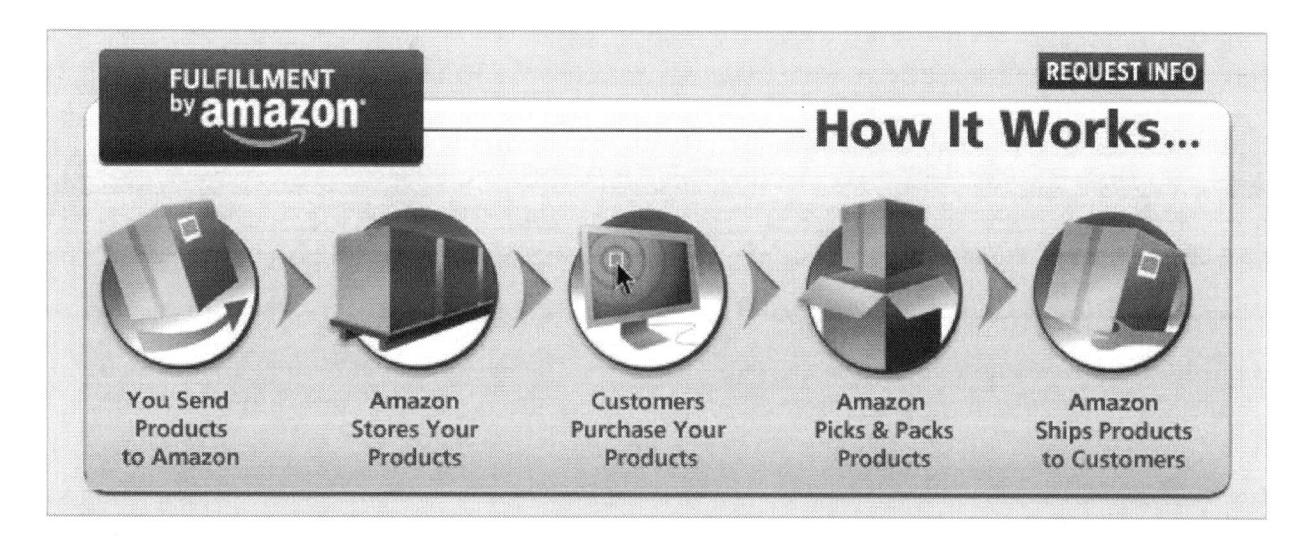

What is FBA? Rather than store the items in your home and ship them yourself (as a lot of eBay sellers do), Amazon lets you ship an entire shipment of new and used items to their warehouses where they store them until they are sold. This is called "Fulfillment by Amazon" (FBA). Once you sell an item, Amazon packs and ships the item and handles all customer service. You can ship to Amazon as often as you like, and while you sleep, they sell your items to targeted buyers.

How does it work? FBA is fairly simple to set up and use, once you get to know the process. Once your seller account is set up, start scanning and listing items. Carefully read the preparation requirements by Amazon. I bag most of my used items per their requirements, and I carefully list any details about flawed items.

Once your items are listed, they are stored in your online database. You select the check-box beside the items you want to send in, click "Change to FBA" and follow the onscreen steps. Amazon will label the items for you for $.20/item (a great deal considering label cost, labor, ink cost, and time!), or, you label the items yourself. Once you approve the shipment, Amazon determines what items are sent to their various warehouses. You print shipping labels right on your home printer, and UPS provides incredibly cheap shipping. All you have to do is measure and weigh the box, print the label, and drop off the box at a UPS store.

Once the items arrive at the Amazon warehouse, the rest is up to them. They promote and advertise your items and keep track of all returns and reimbursements for you. Every two weeks they send you a check for your sales (or you pay in if you have a negative balance due to shipping costs).

What do I sell? It is amazing what you can find around the house to sell. If an item has a barcode, download the "Amazon Seller" app on your phone (or the "Profit Bandit" app), sign in to your Amazon Seller account (fairly simple to set up), scan the barcode and see how much it typically sells for on Amazon. The app details the fees, shipping cost and buy cost; and calculates your profits. It will preview new, used, collectible and other FBA items.

Amazon Prime customers will pay a couple extra dollars to order from an FBA seller over a traditional seller so that they can deal with Amazon's customer service and get the guaranteed 2-day Prime shipping. FBA items typically sell much better than other items, although the fees are slightly higher.

You can start by scanning items around the house to see if it might interest you. I began there and sent my first shipment in days.

Clearance. Other sources for sales with good margins are items on clearance in the stores you regularly shop. Target, Walmart, Kmart, Toys-R-Us, CVS, Walgreen and almost every other store in the world has some kind of clearance section. Either the box has been opened or the store might have overstocked… whatever the reason it is marked WAY down and you can buy it and resell it on Amazon for a profit.

Garage Sales. Each Saturday, I scour garage sales for items to resell. Garage sales have the best profit margins. Examples: a $125 NEW digital photo frame that I bought for $5; a FoodVac that I bought for $3 (profit over $30); a Chia Zombie head I bought for $.50 (profited $12); a $10 lure (profited $25); and scores of board games. I have bought textbooks for $.50 that have sold for $89 (it has happened twice so far); a racecar controller for $5 that sold for $149; and a fountain for $15 that sold for $130 (after the fees, I profited $85. Most board games sell for $15-$20. I found a rare game that sold for $45, and a solid wood Cribbage board that sold for $89. Each of these I got at an estate sale for $1 in a bulk buy (40 games).

Thrift Stores. Each Saturday after door-knocking and the kids' naps, our family goes to Savers Thrift Store. My kids play with the toys and my wife and I scan the board game shelves. People's garage sales are done around noon, and they donate the leftovers to Savers. Savers processes them immediately and we swoop in right in time for first dibs. We usually come away with 15-30 board games, profiting no less than $5 per game (in addition, I find great deals on clothes, too!)

Liquidation Stores. Our town has a liquidation store that purchases truckload shipments (store returns, near expired foods, etc.) and sells the items at discounted rates. Example: I bought 22 breast pumps for $10 each and profited $8 off each one sold (they sell for $27, Amazon takes $9 and I get $18). I have sold cake mix, cake icing, water bottles, sports whistles, eye makeup, lotions and much more from this one store. The benefit of these stores is that you can buy multiple of each of the same item. This means you list it only *once* but add your number of inventory, rather than listing each item individually.

Online. Online liquidation sources like liquidation.com can be a gold mine, as well. Beware of broken items and purchasing on impulse. If you know what you are buying before you order, you can flip the profits quite well. I bought a "baby items" box that sold a ton of stuff almost immediately. I bought a "technology" box that had some cheap items that never sold. Be careful!

Getting Started. Dozens of websites can help get you started with FBA. To get started, I would recommend the following:

- Read the "Getting Started" articles on the Amazon Seller website.
- Sign up for a free seller account at sellercentral.amazon.com (charges $1 per item sold, or choose "pro" for $40/month if you are selling more than 40 items.)
- Download the Amazon Seller App.
- Scan things in your house (board games, cans of food, *anything!*)

More information? Search "FBA" and info will come up all over. Several blogs discuss selling on Amazon as a full-time business.

I follow Pat Flynn on SmartPassiveIncome.com, and one of the guests on his podcast was renowned FBA seller Jessica Larrew. After listening to that podcast (smartpassiveincome.com/session99), I started doing the same. Jessica started small and is now making $100,000 per year on 20 hours per week of work. (She SELLS about $300k, Amazon's fees are about $100k, and she *profits* about $100k.) Her motivation is that anyone can do it. *Visit her blog at* JessicaLarrew.com.

Is this all about the money? I sell through FBA to earn a little side income. I do this in the early mornings for a few hours before work and sometimes in the evenings if I have a big shipment. This is not a full time job, and, for me, it is about earning up a little extra in order to save some money.

Your own philosophy of money can drive *why* you might be interested in doing this.

Conclusion. It has been a fun way to pay for our vacation, buy myself a little work truck and have a few extra bucks in our emergency fund.

You might do it all for missions. You might use it as a fund-raising opportunity for the teens. Whatever the "why," I would encourage you to try it and see if it works for you. It is working for me so far!

Virtual Assistants

What's That? A Virtual Assistant (VA) is the term for an assistant (think: secretary) who works from home. All correspondence is done via the internet through tools like Skype, Email, Dropbox and Bootcamp, and they are paid through online services like PayPal. Many times, VAs are located overseas and can accomplish tasks for you while you sleep.

What Can They Do? While VAs are primarily used in the business setting for people like small business owners who cannot afford to hire a full-time secretary for the bookkeeping, for example, VAs can serve as a valuable time-saver to those in ministry, as well.

From a ministry perspective, hiring a VA (whether they are Christian or not) to serve in the extraneous details of the church is no different than hiring a contractor to build your church building. They provide a service at a cost. It would be similar to paying the light bill. VAs are unseen and not "part of the pastoral ministry team," per se, however, they can provide valuable time-saving service to free you to do things only you can do.

You can give a VA as much or as little input as you desire. Examples of tasks VAs might assist you in:

- Researching and ordering choir music
- Updating class spreadsheets
- Taking and tracking roll
- Attendance reports
- Booking hotels and flights for conferences
- Personal restaurant reservations with a spouse
- Managing your email
- Managing your calendar
- Updating your website
- Posting youth activity pictures to your Facebook page
- Posting announcements
- Posting details of activities
- Setting up email lists for parent lists
- Posting missionary letters on the website
- Research

How Much?

Each business model varies. Some VA services offer a monthly subscription to ALL their VAs, and you can tailor your needs to their expertise. Use a bookkeeper one week, use their graphics designer the next. Use their web designer to set you up a new website then use a General VA to keep it up to date. This model is usually an overseas firm and runs anywhere from $5-$15/hour.

Another model is the freelance model. Prices vary on job type, skill and location of the worker. You can post a single job to freelance sites such as elance.com or odesk.com and receive bids to complete your job. Once you pay the one-time fee, you are done with that project with no monthly fee.

I have used the third model, which is a single, dedicated VA. VirtualStaffFinder.com is a company based in the Philippines. For a one-time fee, they source you with three potential candidates from their pool of talent, matched specifically to your needs. You choose one VA from the three candidates and hire them full time (40 hours *per week*) for a *monthly* fee ranging from $450 - $850 depending on the type of work needed. Part time work cuts the hours and pay in half (20 hours per week, $250+ per month). This VA works her dedicated daily hours on whatever project you determine for her.

More Information. Plenty of information can be found online about how to use VAs and whether it is a good fit for you.

Virtual Freedom (paperback book) is the place to start if you have never heard of and are interested in learning more about VAs. The author Chris Ducker has been a "Virtual CEO" for years now, and he is the founder of VirtualStaffFinder.com. His book has become a best-seller in several categories.

The Virtual Assistant Solution, by Michael Hyatt. EAHelp.com is a virtual Executive Assistant (EA) sourcing company that matches potential clients with quality, experienced, American assistants working from their homes rather than in an office. Michael Hyatt is a nationally-known leader and speaker who is a spokesman for EAHelp and who uses their services. He details in his book the types of ways that an EA can serve, as well as providing some guidelines on how to choose, train and use an EA effectively. It is a short book tailored to a higher-income clientele, although it provides some fabulous ideas for using perhaps a volunteer or person in your church in a virtual setting (working from home and corresponding online).

12. Management Tools

Overseeing various ministries requires tools, communication, and constant refinement. The following list includes some of the tools I currently use (some more than others).

Communication

Slack

I call it "group texting on steroids." Each unique user communicates within channels, and everyone who is invited to that channel can see the whole conversation around that topic. We use church events as channels (#yardsale-2016, for example). Any number of channels, groups, and teams can be created. After the event is over, the channel is archived for future reference, if desired. Our summer team includes 2 interns, 1 church secretary, 1 secretary intern, and me and my wife, and we communicate exclusively through Slack. I communicate with the Heartland Alumni officer team in a completely different window. Direct messages are used in place of text messages, and files are sent through Slack instead of email. The tool includes free apps on all platforms, and notifications can be customized for each channel (e.g. turn OFF notifications for events you are not involved in, but want to be aware of.) Slack is a simple tool with an easy learning curve, and it consolidates a lot of communication tools cleanly.

Trello

Trello features a simple drag/drop interface allowing you to move "cards" between "lists" on a "board" (boards> lists> cards.) If I were to select the Music Ministry "Board," I would see various lists such as "Ideas," "Upcoming," or "Current." The cards on the "Ideas" list might include "Scan choir music" and "purchase more choir music." When we decide to move on an idea, we drag its card to the "Upcoming" or the "Current" list. The tool is simple yet robust, but I rarely use it, personally.

IFTTT

If This Then That creates a set of online triggers with almost any online tool. I use an alert that emails me when anyone adds a new event to our church Google calendar. Do you take iPhone pictures? Do you use Gmail? Do you use Dropbox? Set up IFTTT to download your iOS pictures to DropBox automatically. Have IFTTT send you an email when your "Hue" lights turn on at home. I do not know! You dream it, IFTTT can probably connect it. ifttt.com.

FaceTime (or Skype, or Google Hangout)

Video messaging is good for anything you need to see to make a decision. Rather than text a picture or try to describe it over the phone, use FaceTime instead. Even if it is something that is within your church facilities, use FaceTime rather than in-person "Can you come look at this?" meetings. Want to know if the chairs are set up correctly? Wondering where to hang that picture? Nervous about wiring the ballast correctly? Got a question about the copier? Use FaceTime (or Skype, or Google Hangouts, or any other video conferencing software.)

Jing (Or QuickTime screen capture)

Download Jing for quick and easily sharable screencasts. If you are training an intern or a secretary how to do one of your computer jobs, record and share a screencast of you talking your way through it. For example, if I design our outreach material but have the interns or secretary print them, I can create a screencast of how to change the printer settings to print on glossy, thick paper 16-up 2-sided and color. Use screencasts for how to create a website update, how to lay out an invoice, or how to print a fax cover sheet. Although Jing is free (see techsmith.com/jing), on a Mac, you can instead use the built-in QuickTime screen-capture.

Capture/Organize

Evernote

I took David Allen and Michael Hyatt's advice and now use evernote. David Allen is the author of *Getting Things Done*, which is a methodology that helps you get everything out of your head by writing it down. Michael Hyatt is a Christian leader who is a power user of Evernote. I was previously using Apple's Notes app to capture my thoughts on the go, but now I use Evernote to jot myself notes and store reference material. I have found that its tagging features are the most convenient, so I will write notes as I think of them, tagging them in their particular categories. Example: In my "Secretary" tag on Evernote, I have several different notes on training and using a secretary, job lists I am planning on delegating, ideas for future projects, lists of websites about secretaries and more. In my "Interns" tag, I store my interview notes, some ideas for a book, our church's philosophies and more. I use Evernote first to CAPTURE the thought (into my general "Ryanrench" notebook) and then TAG after that.

Inbox

David Allen's *Getting Things Done (GTD)* methodology and book encourage the user to get everything out of their head and into a system that works for them and that they will regularly review. The first step is CAPTURING every thought that comes through the mind. Neurological studies show that the brain subconsciously exerts energy remembering "undone" things, and it brings those things to our conscious mind unless it trusts that we will be reminded of them some other way in the future. In essence, GTD teaches you to clear your mind by capturing all those loose thoughts and organizing them into a system you trust. Your brain is NOT a good storage container, but it IS good at coming up with new ideas. Our systems should be our storage container, so we should capture everything that is in our mind and put it into our system.

Enter the inbox. David Allen uses the inbox for *everything*. Everything first goes into the inbox, and later gets processed into the system from there. Get to **inbox zero** daily by deciding what to do with every item in the inbox. Have a stack of business cards in your desk drawer? Put them in your inbox, and then force yourself to decide what the **next action** is on each card. Throw it away? Call that person back? Enter it into your rolodex or contact list? Decide! How about that note on the back of Sunday's bulletin? Put it in the inbox. Capture EVERYTHING – every coat pocket, every desk drawer, every cabinet... everything. And then decide.

Once you have hit the first round, for the rest of your life, do that same process with everything. Use your inbox (digital inboxes like email, Facebook, etc.) to capture and then decide what to do with each piece of information.

File Sharing

Google Drive

In my perfect dream world, our entire church server is on Google Drive. We are not there yet, but we are getting there. Google Drive stores documents online, allows you to edit them online, saves them automatically, lets you share them with other users, and best of all—it is FREE. If you use Microsoft Word, Excel, or PowerPoint for basic documents, Google's versions of these programs are similar. I primarily use Google Drive for any document I update regularly and collaborate on. Example: Our Preaching Rally spreadsheet is updated annually by several different secretaries, each doing their own jobs (some are doing mailing, some verifying addresses, some are calling, some are registering, etc.) This spreadsheet is shared with each one and I can see in real time on my screen what they are typing as they type it. Another shared document is my Music Spreadsheet to track all my congregational songs, special music, choir songs, choir books, dates, and much more. Several different people are shared on that document.

Since my internet browser is always open, Google Drive is much faster at creating a quick spreadsheet than opening Microsoft Excel. And, once I close the document in Drive, it is accessible from anywhere I have internet connection and on apps on my phone.

Google Drive's robust, free features are incredible. You can upload Word docs, Excel docs and PDFs, which it then scans and turns into text (OCR capabilities). And did I mention it is free? Love it.

Dropbox

Ok, I love Dropbox, too. I use Dropbox for basically ALL of my active files. Because I am away from the files at the office when I am home, I now store almost everything I can on Dropbox. My weekly teen announcement sheets, my Bible class notes, my orders of service, my entire sermon archive, my church announcements, and even my iPhone photos and Mac's screenshots are stored in Dropbox. Dropbox uploads everything to the cloud and keeps every device that is signed into that account perfectly synced. It is free for an account, and additional space can be earned by sharing references. Go to dropbox.com to learn more, or visit cbctemecula.org/DropRR to sign up for a new account (it will help me earn more space).

LastPass

LastPass and 1Password (among others including Apple's Keychain) are password storing keys. You log into one account (remembering only ONE password), and inside that account you store all your other account passwords. I use LastPass to fill in all those online address forms, input my debit card information, create intense passwords for new sites I log into, store my wife and kids' Social Security information and more. Since it is secured online, I can access it from anywhere as long as I remember my one password. LastPass also has browser extensions that can automatically log you into the websites that you have stored, or it can offer to generate or remember passwords for each website you visit. It is as secure as anything else online, so if you trust your banking online, you can trust LastPass and others like it. It has made my life SO much simpler and keeps getting better as my wife and I share and grow our logins vault.

Scanner Pro (by Readdle)

Scanner apps let you take a picture of a document and in a few seconds you have a PDF that you can then email or save to your computer. With Scanner Pro you can save the file to Dropbox. I use these scanner apps for all kinds of things: getting sheet music onto my iPad, emailing registration forms others need to sign, scanning a page of text and using Google Drive's OCR function so I do not have to re-type the whole page, and more.

Genius Scan

This scanner app is similar to Scanner Pro, but the free version is more limited in its functionality. Both scanners work extremely well, though.

Email Management Ideas

Inbox Zero

Google search "Inbox Zero" and you'll see apps, articles and ads for anything and everything to help you get your inbox under control. I try to practice "Inbox zero" a few different ways.

Two Minute Rule. If it can be done in 2 minutes or less, do it.

If not, decide. Is it an action? Put it on an action list somewhere. (i.e. @home, @office, @phone, or @computer)

If it is reference material, label and archive it. Do not keep it in your inbox. Use Gmail (or any other email service) and archive your message rather than delete it.

If possible, delegate. If you cannot DO it or DECIDE where to file it or when to do it, forward it to whomever can finish it.

Gmail

I love Gmail. I route ALL my email addresses through my Gmail account (I have about 15). Our shared docs are on Google Drive and our church calendar is on Google calendar. Gmail handles spam almost perfectly, and it learns as it goes, so it only gets better over time. In addition, you are given 15GB of FREE storage! This includes every email ever sent with every attachment included. Remember that banner you sent to the guy 3 years ago for VBS? It is in your archives. Type one word from the email in your search bar and it will show up in date order, with the banner graphic still attached! (I do not know HOW many times people email me for songs, announcement sheets, or graphics files. If only they used "archive" instead of "delete" on their email.)

Multiple Inboxes

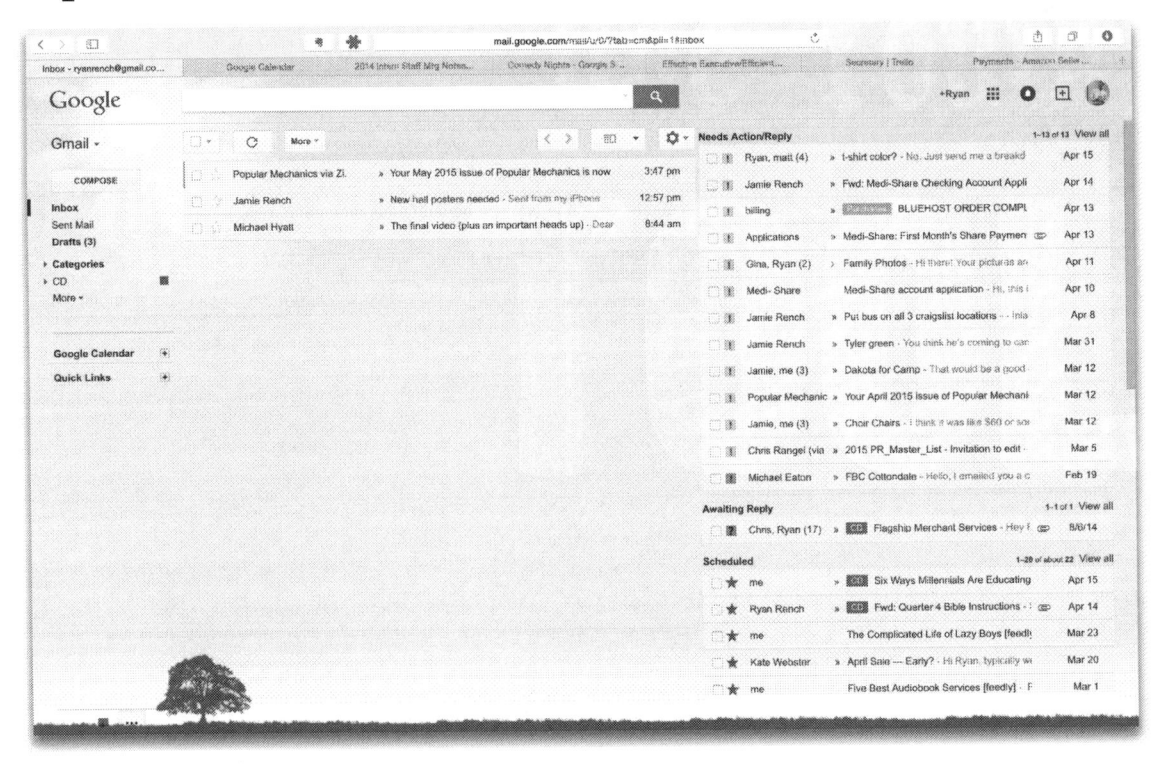

If you have Gmail, one of the labs allows you to have multiple Gmail inboxes open at once (not the same as "Priority Inbox" tabs. Search Google for how to set these up). I route ALL my mail into my one inbox, then label each email individually where I would like it to end up. I use the different color labels to indicate the following: Needs action, Awaiting Reply, Scheduled, Delegated.

If you use Google Chrome as your browser, there are scores of tools that do many of these things automatically. I love the Chrome browser, but I am so entrenched in Apple's system that the Safari browser makes more sense for me to use.

Keyboard Shortcuts

I figure if we are on our computers all day, it makes sense to be able to use them efficiently. Here is a chart of keyboard shortcuts I use almost daily:

Drive your computer from your keyboard. The more you can do without using a mouse or trackpad, the faster you can become. Here are a few keyboard shortcuts I use almost every single day. Many shortcuts cross application boundaries, while others are specific only to that one app. Learn and practice as many as you can.

CURSOR
cmd [arrows] - beginning or end of line or paragraph

opt [arrows] - jump words

DELETING
opt Del - delete a word

cmd Del - delete line

SELECTING
shift [arrows] - highlight words

tab (or shift/tab) - selection boxes

cmd a - select all

TYPING
cmd i - italicize

cmd b - bold

cmd u - underline

[cmd shift <] - decrease font size

[cmd shift >] - increase font size

cmd c - copy

cmd x - cut

cmd v - paste

APPLICATIONS
cmd w - close window

cmd q - quit app

cmd f - find

cmd o - open

cmd s - save

cmd shift s - save as

cmd p - print

cmd z - undo

cmd n - new

cmd [comma] - app preferences

cmd tab - switch apps

cmd ` (by #1) - switch windows

cmd [spacebar] - spotlight (search for anything)

BROWSER
cmd L - search bar

ctrl tab (or ctrl shift tab) - switch tabs

cmd r - refresh

cmd t - open new tab

WORD
cmd 1 - single line spacing

cmd 2 - double line spacing

cmd 5 - 1.5 line spacing

FINDER
opt [up] or [down] - top or bottom of list

cmd [down] - open file

[enter] - change filename

[spacebar] - quick view

SCREENSHOTS
cmd shift 4 - select screenshot

cmd shift 3 - full screen screenshot

Made in the USA
Middletown, DE
18 February 2018